MENDED

HEART

A Woman's Healing Journey with God

LASHANA LLOYD

MENDED HEART

A Woman's Healing Journey with God

by

LaShana Lloyd

Int. Copyright @ 2023 CI-494083246
ISBN: 979-8-218-31040-0
Published in the United States of America

DEDICATION

This journal, "Mended Heart: A Woman's Healing Journey with God," is lovingly dedicated to all the resilient women who have faced the trials of life with courage, faith, and unwavering determination. May these pages serve as a source of hope, healing, and divine inspiration as you embark on your own unique journey toward wholeness and restoration.

Just as a mended heart is often stronger than before, may your faith in God's boundless love and grace lead you to newfound strength and joy. Your story is a testament to the power of faith, and it is an honor to stand with you on this amazing path of healing.

TABLE OF CONTENTS

INTRODUCTION

Welcome to "Mended Heart," a helpful and hopeful space for women on an amazing journey of healing, faith, and restoration. In the coming and going of life, we often find ourselves carrying the weight of our wounds, longing for peace and comfort. This journal is your companion through a life-changing 31-day journey, a walk toward healing guided by the unwavering love of God.

Each day, you will embark on a spiritual journey designed to nurture your heart and spirit while igniting your faith. "Mended Heart: A Woman's Healing Journey with God" includes daily instructions that combine faith-based reflections, guided self-reflection, scriptures, personal testimonials, and prayerful guidance, all intended to guide you toward the direction of renewal and reconciliation in God.

"Throughout this journal, you'll find scriptures that offer wisdom, hope, and reassurance, anchoring your healing process in God's Word."

Let His Word be your steadfast companion as you navigate the challenges and triumphs on your journey.

INTRODUCTION

Faith-Based Reflections:

Begin each day with an inspiring scripture or devotion that sets the tone for your healing journey. As the sun rises, allow these words to resonate in your heart and set the course for the day ahead.

Guided Self-Reflections:

Thoughtful prompts encourage you to explore your emotions, seek God's guidance, and find comfort in His love. This thoughtful part of the journey will help you uncover the depths of your feelings, allowing God's love to saturate your soul.

Scriptures:

Throughout this journal, you'll find verses that offer wisdom, hope, and reassurance, anchoring your healing process in God's Word. Let His Word be your steadfast companion as you navigate the challenges and triumphs on your journey.

Personal Testimonials:

Read uplifting stories from LaShana Lloyd and others who have walked a similar path, finding strength and healing through their faith in God. These narratives of resilience and faith will inspire and uplift you on your own healing journey.

INTRODUCTION

Prayerful Guidance:

Spaces for prayer and gratitude invite you to connect with God, surrender your burdens, and find peace in His plan. In these moments of reflection and connection, you'll discover the power of surrender and the comfort of His grace.

This journal is more than just pages and words, it's a place where your heart will be mended, forming a deeper connection with God, and experiencing the transforming power of faith.

Through the gentle guidance of "Mended Heart: A Woman's Healing Journey with God," you will find healing, hope, and strength in God's love.

As you begin this 31-day journey, may your heart be mended, and your spirit be renewed. The path to healing with God awaits, and each day is a step closer to the restoration you need. Embrace the journey, the healing, and the love of God.

CHAPTER ONE

THE EMOTIONAL CUP

This chapter begins your great journey, with exploring the concept of your emotional cup. Your emotional cup symbolizes your soul, where you hold and process your mind, will, and emotions.

Imagine your emotional cup as a vessel within you, a reservoir that collects every emotion, both joyful and challenging, from your life's journey. It is where you store your memories, hurts, fears, joys, and hopes. This cup is an integral part of who you are, and its contents influence how you experience the world around you.

Before we dive into the practices of faith-based reflection, guided self-reflection, scriptures, personal testimonials, and prayerful guidance, it is essential to understand the state of your emotional cup. What do you currently carry within it? What emotions have filled your cup to the brim, perhaps even spilling over?

In your emotional cup, you might find lingering wounds from past experiences, fears of the unknown, and the weight of unresolved emotions. As you begin this journey, it is crucial to acknowledge the contents of your cup, for only by recognizing what resides within can you begin the healing process.

With acknowledging your emotional cup, you take the first step towards mending your heart. You acknowledge that you are a vessel capable of renewal, transformation, and healing through your faith in God. This is not a journey to discard your emotions, but to cleanse, renew, and replenish them with the blessings of faith.

As we progress through the days ahead, we will learn to empty the cup of what no longer serves us, gently releasing the pain, regret, and burdens that have weighed us down. We will fill your emotional cup with the balm of faith-based reflection, guided self-reflection, scriptures, personal testimonials, and prayerful guidance. The process of emptying and filling is similar to a transformation that changes your heart and soul.

As a garden needs tending to flourish, so does your emotional cup. In the days to come, we will nurture your inner garden, allowing the seeds of faith to bloom and the waters of grace to flow. Once heavy and burdensome, your emotional cup will become a vessel of renewal and healing, holding the sweet nectar of God's love and compassion.

As you embrace this first chapter of your journey, take a moment to reflect on what your emotional cup contains. What would you like to release, and what would you like to invite in? Remember that this is a journey of renewal, and by the end of it, your emotional cup will be transformed into a vessel of mended and overflowing love, faith, and healing.

THE EMOTIONAL CUP

We all have the capacity to absorb excellent and sad emotions within our brains. When our emotional role is full of negative emotions, further negative emotions result in an overspill, as seen in various behaviors.

Look at the diagram below. In our lives, we experience many hurts that can accumulate if not dealt with at the time. The damage is more challenging when it comes from those we don't expect to hurt us, such as family members, church members, friends, business partners, teachers, and other people we trust (See section on forgiveness).

We tend to focus on dealing with the SYMPTOMS of the full emotional cup, which will provide only temporary relief (e.g., pills for dealing with depression, sleeping pills, addiction programmers, etc.) when, instead, we need to focus on dealing with the CAUSES which will stop the cup overflowing in the first place.

EXERCISE

So, How Do We Empty The Emotional Cup?

- If you are hurting, you will need comforting
- If you are angry, you need to forgive
- If you feel guilty, you need to apologize
- If you experience low self-esteem or a sense of false guilt, you need to hear the truth spoken to you. For example, you may be accused of being useless. Fine, you may have failed at one specific point, like everyone else, but that does not make you worthless in general. It would be best if you heard positive messages rather than blanket condemnation.
- If you are fearful, you need to receive love
- If you are stressed, you need to gain support

PLEASE VIEW THE EXAMPLE ON THE NEXT PAGE

SYMPTOMS OF A FULL CUP

Depressed Mood

Escape into work, drugs, infidelity, pornography, etc

Impatience, quick temper

Loss of energy & concentration.

Physical side effects

Loss of emotions like joy, love, affection & romance

Sleep & appetite disturbance

Stress
Anxiety
Fears
Insecurities
False Guilt
Condemnation
True Guilt
Retaliation
Anger
Bitterness &
Resentment
Hurt

Our emotional capacity

Unhealthy Accumulation of negative Emotions

Unmet needs increase

CHRONIC PAIN AND OTHER ILLNESS, ALLERGIES, FATIGUE

LOSS OF ENERGY AND CONCENTRATION

ESCAPE INTO WORK, ALCOHOL, DRUGS, PORN, FANTASY, TV, INTERNET

LOSS OF POSITIVE EMOTIONS SUCH AS JOY, LOVE, AFFECTION AND ROMANCE

DEPRESSION AND LOW MOOD

IMPATIENCE, QUICK TEMPER, ANGRY

SLEEP AND APPETITE DISTURBANCE

STRESS
ANGER   BITTERNESS RESENTMENT
FEAR   ANXIETY
HURT   GRIEF
SHAME   PAIN
GUILT
ENVY
JEALOUSY

UNHEALTHY ACCUMULATION OF NEGATIVE EMOTIONS

Once these feelings come to the surface from being suppressed, a healing process takes place, and you can be free. There will be some scriptures in the first-person noun, which you can repeat out loud. After repenting, ask the Lord to heal you from all hurt, harm, and danger and forgive yourself!

In many situations, the devil wants us to carry unforgiveness, hurt, emotional wounds and not trust anyone. It is the Lord's will that none of us perish, but we all come to repentance (2 Peter 3:9).

So, once applied, these scriptures will heal, deliver, and set you free. When you begin to repeat these scriptures, take deep breaths. Breathe in through your nose and release through your mouth, because demonic spirits are attached through our nasal passage.

I pray this book becomes a blessing for you and a tool in your library you use daily until you are entirely and ultimately set free by the hands of the Almighty God, in Jesus' name.

DAY 1

TITLE: <u>Emotional Trauma</u>   **DATES:_____**

SCRIPTURE REFERENCE

Psalm 56:8 (NLT)
"You keep track of all my sorrows. You have collected all my tears in your bottle. You have recorded each one in your book."

SPIRITUAL THOUGHT

As we begin this healing journey, starting with unpacking the weight of emotional trauma, let this scripture remind us of God's unwavering presence, especially in our moments of brokenness. Just as a loving parent is close to their hurting child, God is near us, ready to save and heal.

SCRIPTURES OF THE DAY

Throughout this healing journey, we will draw wisdom, hope, and reassurance from the Word of God. Let these verses anchor your healing process:

"He heals the brokenhearted and binds up their wounds."
Psalm 147:3 (NIV)

"Come to me, all you who are weary and burdened, and I will give you rest."
Matthew 11:28 (NIV)

GUIDED SELF-REFLECTION

Today, take some time for self-reflection as we dive into the depths of our emotional trauma

1. Acknowledging the Pain: Think back to the moment when you first felt the weight of your emotional trauma. What were the circumstances, emotions, and reactions you experienced? Acknowledge and write down these feelings.

----

2. The Impact on Your Life: Reflect on how this emotional trauma has affected different aspects of your life. Consider your relationships, self-esteem, daily routines, and overall well-being.

GUIDED SELF-REFLECTION

3. What Healing Means to You: Define what healing looks like for you. How would your life be different if you were able to release the emotional burden and find restoration? Write down your aspirations for healing.

TESTIMONIAL

Mary, the mother of Jesus, indeed experienced significant emotional trauma throughout her life. Her journey as the mother of the Messiah was marked by extraordinary events and challenges that brought emotional turmoil and heartache. Here are some key aspects of the emotional trauma Mary faced:

1. The Announcement and Unexpected Pregnancy:

Mary's story begins with the angel Gabriel's visit, announcing that she would conceive a child through the Holy Spirit. While this event was a profound spiritual experience, it also brought tremendous fear, confusion, anxiety, and emotional turmoil. Imagine the emotional weight of being chosen for such a divine task, knowing that many would see her pregnancy as illegitimate and possibly subject her to societal ostracism. Mary had to deal with the internal and external conflicts this revelation brought.

2. Social Humiliation and Public Scrutiny:

In a conservative society, Mary's pregnancy out of wedlock would have exposed her to her community's harsh judgment and social embarrassment. The emotional trauma of being misunderstood, judged, and possibly rejected by her community, and even her own family, must have been excruciating. She would have had to endure the whispers, the disapproving looks, and the potential isolation.

3. The Sudden Departure to Egypt:

After Jesus' birth, Mary and Joseph fled to Egypt to escape King Herod's decree to kill all infants. The emotional trauma of leaving one's homeland, possibly losing friends and family, and living as refugees in a foreign land would have left a lasting impact. The fear for her child's safety would have been a constant cause of anxiety.

4. Loss of Jesus in the Temple:

When Jesus was twelve years old, Mary and Joseph lost him in Jerusalem while they were on a pilgrimage. The confusion and distress Mary must have experienced during this incident would have been emotionally traumatic because the panic and fear a parent experiences when their child goes missing is a traumatizing event. Finding Jesus in the temple was a mixture of relief and concern for his well-being.

5. Witnessing the Crucifixion of Jesus:

Perhaps the most significant emotional trauma Mary endured was witnessing her Son's crucifixion. Standing at the foot of the cross, Mary observed the horrific and brutal execution of Jesus. To see her child subjected to such a brutal and public execution would have been an unimaginable emotional ordeal. The helplessness of being unable to protect or comfort her child in His final moments must have left deep emotional scars.

As the mother of Jesus, Mary's journey was filled with moments of great privilege and suffering. Her emotional trauma and challenges were a testament to her strength and faith. Despite the immense pain she experienced, Mary remained steadfast in her love and devotion to her Son, and her role in the story of salvation is a powerful example of faith and resilience in the face of emotional trauma. Her journey as the mother of Jesus is a reminder that even in the most challenging circumstances, one can find strength and grace to endure, guided by love and faith. Mary's story continues to inspire empathy and compassion for those who face trauma, discrimination, and hardship in their lives.

PRAYER GUIDANCE

PRAYER FOR EMOTIONAL TRAUMA

Dear Heavenly Father, I come before You with a heart heavy with the weight of my emotional trauma. I acknowledge the pain I've carried, the scars that have formed, and its impact on my life. Lord, I seek your guidance on this healing journey.

As I reflect on my experiences, I surrender them to Your divine care. I ask for the strength to let go of the burdens that have held me captive for so long. Fill me with Your love, grace, and peace as I take these initial steps toward healing.

Help me define what healing means and grant me the wisdom to see the path You have set before me. May I find comfort in Your love and the assurance that You are close to the brokenhearted, just as You are close to me. I place my trust in Your divine plan for my healing in Jesus' name.

Amen

In the space provided, offer a prayer to God, laying your burdens before Him:

May this Day 1 entry begin a life-changing path toward healing your mended heart. You are not alone, and through faith, reflection, prayer, and the Word of God, there is hope for your healing and restoration.

DAY 2

TITLE: <u>Fear</u>   **DATES:** _____

SCRIPTURE REFERENCE

2 Timothy 1:7 (KJV)
"For God hath not given us the spirit of fear; but of power, love, and a sound mind."

SPIRITUAL THOUGHT

We turn to God's Word for guidance and comfort on our journey to heal us from fear. His presence is a source of support and reassurance in times of uncertainty.

SCRIPTURES OF THE DAY

Draw wisdom, hope, and reassurance from these verses:

"When I am afraid, I put my trust in you."
Psalm 56:3 (NIV)

"I sought the LORD, and he answered me and delivered me from all my fears."
Psalm 34:4 (ESV)

GUIDED SELF-REFLECTION

As you embark on this day of exploring your fears, take a moment for self-reflection:

1. **Identifying Your Fears**: What specific fears or anxieties have weighed your heart and mind? Write them down, no matter how big or small they may seem.

----

2. **Triggers and Patterns**: Reflect on what triggers these fears and whether you notice any patterns in the situations or thoughts that lead to fear.

----

3. **The Impact of Fear**: Consider how fear has affected your life, from your relationships to your overall well-being. What areas of your life have been most impacted by fear?

TESTIMONIAL

In Genesis 3, Adam and Eve's experience of fear, after eating the forbidden fruit in the Garden of Eden, represents a significant turning point in their relationship with God and their understanding of the world.

After eating the forbidden fruit from the tree of the knowledge of good and evil, Adam and Eve suddenly became aware of their nakedness and felt shame because the serpent tricked them. This newfound self-awareness led to their fear as they realized their vulnerability and the moral consequences of their disobedience.

They hid themselves among the trees when they heard God walking in the garden. This fear of God's presence is a direct consequence of their disobedience. They understood that they had broken God's command and feared the judgment or punishment they might face.

They hid themselves among the trees when they heard God walking in the garden. This fear of God's presence is a direct consequence of their disobedience. They understood that they had broken God's command and feared the judgment or punishment they might face.

Their fear also led to a sense of separation from God. Before eating the forbidden fruit, they had enjoyed a close, pleasant relationship with God, walking with Him in the garden. However, their disobedience created a division, both emotionally and spiritually. They no longer felt the same level of intimacy and trust in God.

TESTIMONIAL

When God questioned them about their actions, both Adam and Eve attempted to shift the blame. Adam blamed Eve, and Eve blamed the serpent. This blame-shifting can be seen as an attempt to alleviate their fear of God's anger and judgment by deflecting responsibility.

Their fear had consequences, as God pronounced punishments for their actions. Adam and Eve would now face hardships and struggles, and they were banished from the Garden of Eden, losing the amazing paradise they had enjoyed.

The fear experienced by Adam and Eve, in the aftermath of eating the forbidden fruit, reflects the human condition after the introduction of sin into the world. It highlights the complex emotions, spiritual consequences of disobedience, and separation from God. The story of Adam and Eve serves as a foundational narrative, illustrating the human struggle with sin, the need for redemption, and the consequences of straying from God's will.

This is why God sending of Jesus into the world is seen as His response to the sin of Adam and Eve in the Garden of Eden. It provides a path to redemption, reconciliation, and the hope of eternal life for those who accept Jesus as their Savior.

PRAYER GUIDANCE

PRAYER FOR FEAR

Heavenly Father, I come to You today with a heart burdened by fear. I acknowledge the anxieties that have held me captive and the moments when uncertainty overwhelmed me. Lord, grant me the courage to trust in Your love and protection. Help me overcome my fears and face them with faith. May Your presence be my refuge and source of strength. I find the peace that surpasses all understanding in Jesus' name.

Amen

In the space provided, offer a prayer to God, laying your fears before Him:

_____

_____

_____

_____

_____

_____

_____

_____

_____

_____

_____

As you continue your journey towards a mended heart, remember that facing fear is a brave and developing step. You have God's Word, the wisdom of others, and the power of prayer to guide you toward healing and freedom from fear.

DAY 3

TITLE: <u>Brokenness</u>   **DATES:_____**

SCRIPTURE REFERENCE

Psalm 34:18 (NIV)
"The LORD is close to the brokenhearted and saves those who are crushed in spirit."

SPIRITUAL THOUGHT

On our journey toward healing, we recognize that brokenness can be a step toward wholeness.

SCRIPTURES OF THE DAY

Draw wisdom, hope, and reassurance from these verses:

"But we have this treasure in jars of clay to show that the surpassing power belongs to God and not to us."
2 Corinthians 4:7 (ESV)

"The sacrifices of God are a broken spirit; a broken and contrite heart, O God, you will not despise."
Psalm 51:17 (ESV)

GUIDED SELF-REFLECTION

As you navigate this day's exploration of brokenness, take time for self-reflection:

1. Embracing Brokenness: Consider the areas of your life where you have experienced brokenness, whether through past experiences, relationships, or personal struggles.

----

2. Understanding Your Brokenness: Reflect on how brokenness has shaped your character, perspective, and relationship with God. How has it impacted your journey?

----

3. Healing Through Brokenness: Explore the idea that brokenness can be a path to healing and growth. Are there moments when you have found strength and resilience through your brokenness?

TESTIMONIAL

The story of the woman with the issue of blood, as described in Mark 5:25-34 in the Bible, is a powerful narrative of brokenness, desperation, and unwavering faith. The woman had been suffering from a hemorrhage of blood for twelve years. This ailment not only caused her severe physical pain, but also made her ritually unclean according to Jewish law, isolating her from society. She had likely endured countless treatments and medical interventions without any improvement. Her physical suffering led to emotional and psychological brokenness, as she must have felt hopeless and isolated from everyone else.

After enduring this condition for over a decade, the woman had likely reached a point of utter desperation. She had spent all her resources seeking medical help but found no relief. The desperation she felt was not only due to her physical ailment but also the emotional turmoil of being ostracized from her community.

The woman held on to her hope and faith despite her brokenness and despair. She had heard of Jesus' healing miracles and believed that she would be healed if she could just touch the hem of His garment. Her determination and faith were so strong that she was willing to brave the crowds, believing that a simple touch could bring about the healing she sought.

TESTIMONIAL

As the woman reached out to touch the edge of Jesus' garment, she was immediately healed. Jesus felt power go out from Him, and He asked who had touched Him. The woman, trembling with fear, came forward to admit it was her. Jesus responded with compassion and affirmed her faith, by telling her that her faith had made her well.

Through her unwavering faith, the woman experienced physical healing and a restoration of her social and emotional well-being. She was no longer an outcast but could rejoin her community without fear of ritual impurity. Her faith had made her whole in every sense of the word.

The story of the woman with the issue of blood is an important reminder of the power of faith in the face of brokenness and despair. It serves as an example of how faith can lead to healing and restoration. This narrative is a testament to the compassion and miraculous power of Jesus and an inspiration for individuals facing overwhelming challenges to hold onto their faith and hope in their journey toward wholeness.

PRAYER GUIDANCE

PRAYER FOR BROKENNESS

Heavenly Father, I come before You with a heart that carries the weight of brokenness. I acknowledge the moments when life's trials and challenges have left me shattered. Lord, help me understand that You see an opportunity for healing, transformation, and renewal in my brokenness. May I offer my brokenness as a sacred sacrifice trusting that You can make something beautiful from the pieces. I find hope in the midst of brokenness in Jesus' name.

Amen

In the space provided, offer a prayer to God, surrendering your brokenness and seeking His guidance

----

As you continue your journey toward mending your heart, remember that brokenness can be a steppingstone to healing and restoration. You can find strength and renewal in your brokenness through faith, reflection, and prayer.

DAY 4

TITLE: <u>Mother Issues</u>   **DATES:_____**

SCRIPTURE REFERENCE

Exodus 20:12 (ESV)
"Honor your father and your mother, that your days may be long in the land that the Lord your God is giving you."

SPIRITUAL THOUGHT

As we go further into the complexities of mother issues, we look to the commandment that calls us to honor our parents. This verse reminds us of the importance of our relationship with our mothers and the need for healing and reconciliation.

SCRIPTURES OF THE DAY

Find wisdom and reassurance in these verses:

"Listen to your father who gave you life, and do not despise your mother when she is old."
Proverbs 23:22 (ESV)

"A wise son makes a glad father, but a foolish son is a sorrow to his mother."
Proverbs 10:1 (ESV)

GUIDED SELF-REFLECTION

Take time today for self-reflection on your relationship with your mother:

1. Mother's Influence: Reflect on your mother's impact on your life. How has her presence, actions, or words influenced your journey?

----

2. Challenges and Resentments: Consider any challenges or conflicts you have faced with your mother. What resentments or unresolved issues may be affecting your well-being?

----

3. Healing and Forgiveness: Explore the idea of healing and forgiveness in your relationship with your mother. How might forgiveness lead to your own healing?

TESTIMONIAL

The story of Rebekah, the wife of Isaac, and her relationship with her twin sons, Esau and Jacob, highlights a significant mother issue in the Bible involving favoritism, deception, and the profound impact of parental choices on their children's lives.

Rebekah's favoritism towards her younger son, Jacob, is a central theme in their family's story. The Bible tells us that she loved Jacob more than Esau (Genesis 25:28). This favoritism profoundly impacted her children and ultimately led to a cascade of consequences.

Rebekah played a key role in orchestrating a plan to deceive her husband, Isaac, into giving Jacob the blessing intended for the firstborn, Esau (Genesis 27). This act of deception was driven by her desire to see Jacob favored over Esau and fulfill the prophecy she received during her pregnancy. Rebekah's actions, in essence, pitted her sons against each other.

Rebekah's favoritism, and the ensuing deception, caused deep-seated conflict within the family. Esau, feeling cheated out of his birthright, was furious with Jacob. Jacob had to flee to escape Esau's anger, and Rebekah never saw her favored son again. This division tore the family apart.

TESTIMONIAL

The consequences of Rebekah's actions continued for years, impacting the relationships within the family. Jacob's life was marked by struggles and challenges, including his dealings with his uncle Laban, whom he had to deceive. The broken relationships within the family illustrate the long-term repercussions of Rebekah's favoritism and deception.

Rebekah's story serves as a cautionary tale about the responsibilities of parenthood. Her favoritism led to division and suffering, illustrating the profound impact that parents can have on their children's lives. It reminds us of the importance of treating our children fairly and ensuring that our actions and choices as parents are guided by love, wisdom, and integrity.

Rebekah's mother issue, characterized by her favoritism and deception, offers a valuable lesson in the Bible about the complexities of parenting and the enduring consequences of parental actions. It highlights the importance of fairness and equity in relationships with children and the responsibility of parents to guide their children with love and integrity. The story of Rebekah, Esau, and Jacob is a powerful reminder that the choices and actions of parents can profoundly shape family dynamics and relationships.

PRAYER GUIDANCE

PRAYER FOR MOTHER ISSUES

Heavenly Father, I bring the difficulties and tests of my relationship with my mother before You. I acknowledge the impact she has had on my life, both positive and challenging. Lord, help me navigate this journey with grace and wisdom. Guide me in the path of healing and forgiveness. May I find the strength to honor my mother and, in doing so, experience healing in my own heart. I seek Your guidance and peace in Jesus' name.

Amen

In the space provided, offer a prayer to God, seeking His guidance and peace in your relationship with your mother:

_____

_____

_____

_____

_____

_____

_____

_____

_____

_____

_____

As you continue on your healing journey, remember that the mother-child relationships can be complex, but with faith, reflection, and prayer, there is hope for mending and finding peace.

DAY 5

TITLE: <u>Father Issues</u>   **DATES:_____**

SCRIPTURE REFERENCE

Exodus 20:12 (ESV)

"Honor your father and your mother, that your days may be long in the land that the Lord your God is giving you."

SPIRITUAL THOUGHT

On our journey of healing related to father issues, we must understand the importance of a father's role and the need for reconciliation and healing.

SCRIPTURES OF THE DAY

"And because we are his children, God has sent the Spirit of his Son into our hearts, prompting us to call out, "Abba, Father." Now, you are no longer a slave but God's own child. And since you are his child, God has made you his heir."

Galatians 4:6-7 (NLT)

GUIDED SELF-REFLECTION

Take a moment today for self-reflection on your relationship with your Father:

1. Father's Influence: Reflect on your father's impact on your life. How has his presence, actions, or words shaped your journey?

----

2. Challenges and Resentments: Consider any challenges or conflicts you have faced with your father. What resentments or unresolved issues may be affecting your well-being?

----

3. Healing and Forgiveness: Explore the idea of healing and forgiveness in your relationship with your father. How might forgiveness lead to your own healing?

TESTIMONIAL

In the Bible, Leah, Laban's daughter, and Jacob's first wife, is a woman who faced significant father issues, particularly feelings of being unloved by her father, Laban. Her story is found in Genesis and is a sad illustration of the emotional and relational challenges that can arise within families.

Leah's story begins with her father, Laban, orchestrating a trick. Laban promised Jacob that he could marry Rachel, Leah's younger sister, whom Jacob loved. However, Laban substituted Leah for Rachel on the wedding night, and Jacob unknowingly marries Leah instead. This deceit shows a lack of care for Leah's feelings and desires, highlighting her father's preference for Rachel.

Leah's name is significant, meaning "weary" or "grieved." It is an indication of her inner turmoil and the emotional weight she carried throughout her life. She must have felt unloved by her father, as Laban prioritized Rachel and used Leah as a pawn in his dealings with Jacob. This would have caused deep emotional wounds for Leah, contributing to her feelings of inadequacy and unimportance.

TESTIMONIAL

In the midst of her turmoil, the Bible tells us that God saw Leah's situation and had compassion for her. God granted her children and eventually shifted the focus of her love and identity from Jacob to God. This transformation allowed Leah to find a sense of self-worth and fulfillment beyond the approval of her father.

Leah's story in the Bible is a helpful reminder of the emotional toll that can result from feeling unloved or unwanted by one's own father. Her journey is one of transformation, as she ultimately finds her value not in the love of a man, but in her relationship with God and in her role as a mother. Her story serves as a testament to the power of faith and resilience in the face of challenging family dynamics and emotional wounds.

PRAYER GUIDANCE

PRAYER FOR FATHER ISSUES

Heavenly Father, I bring before You the problems and challenges of my relationship with my father. I acknowledge the impact he has had on my life, both good and concerning. Lord, help me navigate this journey with grace and wisdom. Guide me in the path of healing and forgiveness. May I find the strength to honor my father and, in doing so, experience healing in my own heart. I seek Your guidance and peace in Jesus' name.

Amen

In the space provided, offer a prayer to God, seeking His guidance and peace in Your relationship with your father:

As you continue your healing journey, remember that the difficulties of a father-daughter relationship can be trying. However, with faith, reflection, and prayer, there is hope for mending and finding peace.

DAY 6

TITLE: <u>**Overcoming Rejection**</u>   **DATES:**_____

SCRIPTURE REFERENCE

Psalm 139:14 (NIV)

Scripture of the Day: "I praise you because I am fearfully and wonderfully made; your works are wonderful; I know that full well."

SPIRITUAL THOUGHT

On this day of your healing journey, we dive into the emotions of rejection, self-doubt, insecurity, and low self-esteem, seeking to find healing and restoration.

SCRIPTURES OF THE DAY

Find hope and encouragement in these verses that remind you of your worth in the eyes of your Creator:

"But the LORD said to Samuel, "Do not consider his appearance or height, for I have rejected him. The LORD does not look at the things people look at. People look at the outward appearance, but the LORD looks at the heart."
1 Samuel 16:7 (KJV)

"You are precious and honored in my sight, and I love you."
Isaiah 43:4 (NIV)

GUIDED SELF-REFLECTION

Today's self-reflection invites you to explore your experiences with rejection, self-perception, and self-esteem:

1. **Rejection and Its Impact:** Reflect on moments of rejection in your life, whether by others or self-inflicted. How have these experiences shaped your self-esteem and self-worth?

----

2. **Discovering Your Intrinsic** Value: Consider what it means to be "fearfully and wonderfully made" in God's image. How can you embrace and truly believe in your value as a child of God?

----

3. **Overcoming Insecurities:** Identify specific insecurities you struggle with and consider how your faith can help you overcome them. How can your faith empower you to reject negative self-perceptions?

TESTIMONIAL

Rejection threw a dark shadow over my life. It's a darkness that moved into my self-esteem, relationships, and my overall sense of self-worth. The rejection of others, and even more painfully, self-rejection, held me captive for a long time.

For as long as I can remember, I struggled with rejection. It's an emotion that can cut deeper than any blade, leaving scars that are invisible to the naked eye, but engraved deeply into the soul. It comes from the enemy as a whisper in your mind that constantly reminds you that you're not good enough, not worthy of love, and destined to be an outcast.

The seeds of rejection were sown early in my life, perhaps even before I was fully aware. The playground taunts, the unkind words, and the dismissive gestures left me with a sense of unworthiness. As I grew older, these early experiences shaped the lens through which I saw the world. I began to anticipate rejection in a lot of interactions, building walls around my heart to protect myself from the pain.

The most deceptive form of rejection is self-rejection. The constant, internal voice from the enemy tells you that you're not good enough, smart enough, attractive enough, etc. It's the belief that you don't deserve happiness or love because of your perceived flaws. For years, I let this self-rejection dictate my choices and limit my potential.

TESTIMONIAL

But today, I stand as a living testament to the life-changing power of faith and God's healing grace. I found comfort in the darkest hour of my life by turning to God, who saw me not as a rejected soul but as a beloved child of His creation. I realized that God's love was unconditional and could pierce through the darkest places that had clouded my heart.

Through prayer and faith, I learned to forgive those who had rejected me, and most importantly, I learned to forgive myself. I was able to let go of the past and embrace the present with open arms. As I sought God's guidance, I discovered the strength to break free from the chains of rejection and insecurity that had held me captive for so long.

God's healing power flowed through me, mending the broken pieces of my self-esteem, relationships, and self-worth. It was a process, but each day brought a new layer of healing and restoration. I began to see myself through the lens of God's love, which revealed my true worth and purpose.

Today, I stand before you, not as a victim of rejection, but as a survivor whom God's love has transformed. My journey is a testimony to His unending mercy and grace. I know now that I am worthy, loved and can face any darkness with faith and courage. Rejection may have, at one point and time in my life, cast darkness over my life, but with God's healing and deliverance, that shadow has been banished, and I walk in the light of His love.

PRAYER GUIDANCE

PRAYER FOR OVERCOMING REJECTION

Heavenly Father, I come before You with my experiences of rejection, self-doubt, and insecurity. Help me to see myself as You see me, fearfully and wonderfully made in Your image. Strengthen my self-esteem and self-worth through the power of Your love and grace. Guide me as I navigate these emotions and empower me to break free from the chains of insecurity. Grant me the confidence to embrace my identity as Your child and to recognize my value. I pray for Your guidance on this aspect of my healing journey in Jesus' name.

Amen

In the space provided, offer a prayer to God, seeking His guidance in overcoming rejection, self-doubt, insecurity, and low self-esteem.

May this Day 6 entry help you confront feelings of rejection and insecurity, nurturing a healthier self-esteem rooted in the love and acceptance of our Creator.

DAY 7

TITLE: <u>Healing from Church Hurt</u>   **DATES:** _____

SCRIPTURE REFERENCE

Colossians 3:13 (NIV)

"Bear with each other and forgive one another if any of you has a grievance against someone. Forgive as the Lord forgave you."

SPIRITUAL THOUGHT

As you continue your healing journey, today focuses on the pain of church hurt. Let's seek understanding, forgiveness, and renewal.

SCRIPTURES OF THE DAY

Draw wisdom and comfort from these verses, which emphasize forgiveness and the healing power of God's love:

"Don't repay evil for evil. Don't retaliate with insults when people insult you. Instead, pay them back with a blessing. God has called you to do that, and he will grant you his blessing."
1 Peter 3:9 (NLT)

"The Lord is close to the brokenhearted and saves those who are crushed in spirit."
Psalm 34:18 (NIV)

GUIDED SELF-REFLECTION

Today's self-reflection encourages you to explore your experiences with church hurt and find a path toward healing:

1. **Understanding the Hurt:** Reflect on any experiences in your church or faith community that have caused you pain. What aspects of these experiences were particularly hurtful?

----

2. **Unpacking Emotions:** Explore the emotions you've felt in the wake of church hurt. Have you felt anger, betrayal, sadness, or confusion? How have these emotions affected your faith journey?

----

3. **The Path to Forgiveness:** Consider the power of forgiveness, both in the context of your faith and as a means of healing from church hurt. How can you begin to forgive those who may have caused you pain?

TESTIMONIAL

Church hurt is a deeply personal and often unspoken experience, and I have experienced the strength and resilience of it as I navigated this challenging journey. Church hurt was a painful chapter in my life, but it has ultimately strengthened my relationship with God and deepened my faith. It's a reminder that even in this, the love of God can shine through, and we can find healing and renewal. My story is a testament to the power of healing and growth within the church community.

Before my journey of healing, I carried the heavy burden of church hurt. I had experienced disappointment, betrayal, and emotional wounds within the church environment, a place that should ideally be a source of spiritual nourishment, support, and belonging. These experiences left deep scars on my faith and sense of trust.

The wounds of church hurt ran deep. I felt abandoned and deeply disappointed. I questioned my faith, trust in people, and even my own worth. The pain of betrayal and rejection was sometimes unbearable, and I contemplated leaving the church altogether.

TESTIMONIAL

Despite the pain I endured, I chose not to let church hurt define my journey with God and Jesus Christ. Instead, I turned to a combination of self-reflection, prayer, and a supportive community to help me heal and develop my relationship and faith in God.

The healing process was not quick or easy. It required forgiveness, not only for those who had caused the hurt, but also for myself. I needed to forgive my own feelings of anger and resentment. I found strength in scripture, which reminded me of God's grace, mercy, and the importance of forgiveness in the face of pain. The more I leaned on my faith, the more I felt God's presence and the warmth of His love, even in the midst of church hurt.

Slowly but surely, the wounds began to mend. As I forgave and let go of the bitterness that had held me captive, I discovered a renewed sense of purpose and a deeper connection with God and my faith. I realized that the imperfections of some people in the church did not define my relationship with God, and I could always find Him when I needed Him.

TESTIMONIAL

Today, I stand as a living testimony of resilience and faith. My journey through church hurt has strengthened my spiritual connection and deepened my understanding of the true teachings of my faith. I've chosen to use experiences as a source of sympathy, compassion, and support for others who may be going through similar struggles.

My story serves as a reminder that church hurt, while painful, does not have to be the end of one's journey with God. My resilience and ability to heal and forgive are a testament to the power of faith and the human spirit. It is a story of hope and redemption, a light for anyone who may be navigating the rough road of church hurt, showing that healing and growth are possible, even in the face of hardship.

PRAYER GUIDANCE

PRAYER FOR HEALING FROM CHURCH HURT

Father, I bring the pain I've experienced through church hurt before You. Help me to understand the hurt, navigate my emotions, and begin the journey of forgiveness. As I reflect on Your Word, guide me toward the path of healing. Remind me of Your love and Your closeness to the brokenhearted. Grant me the strength to forgive as You have forgiven me. May Your peace fill my heart as I seek renewal in my faith journey. I pray for healing and deliverance from church hurt in Jesus' name.

Amen

In the space provided, offer a prayer to God, seeking His guidance in healing from church hurt:

May this Day 7 entry provide you with the tools to begin healing from the pain of church hurt, allowing you to renew your connection with your faith and your community.

DAY 8

TITLE: <u>Barrenness</u>   **DATES:** _____

SCRIPTURE REFERENCE

Exodus 23:26 (ESV)

"None shall miscarry or be barren in your land; I will fulfill the number of your days."

SPIRITUAL THOUGHT

As we explore the deep pain of barrenness, let this scripture remind us of God's power to bring joy and peace to those who face this journey.

SCRIPTURES OF THE DAY

Anchor your journey with these scriptures:

"For nothing will be impossible with God."
Luke 1:37 (ESV)

"I waited patiently for the Lord; he inclined to me and heard my cry."
Psalm 40:1 (ESV)

GUIDED SELF-REFLECTION

Today, we turn our hearts to the emotional struggle of barrenness. Take time to reflect on your experience:

1. Acknowledging the Pain: Reflect on the emotions you've felt in your journey through barrenness. Acknowledge the pain, disappointment, and longing that you've experienced. Write down these feelings.

----

2. God's Plan and Timing: Contemplate the concept of God's plan and His timing. How do you view your situation from a perspective of faith? How might God be at work in your life through this challenge?

----

3. Hope and Healing: Define what hope and healing mean to you in the context of barrenness. What steps can you take to find hope and healing in your heart?

TESTIMONIAL

Hannah's deep desire for children, and her inability to conceive, caused her immense emotional distress. In her society, being childless was often seen as a source of shame and social stigma. Her anguish is evident in her interactions with her husband, Elkanah, and her rival, Peninnah. Peninnah, who had children, would taunt and provoke Hannah, worsening her emotional pain.

Hannah's response to her barrenness was to pour out her heart to God in fervent prayer. She went to the tabernacle at Shiloh and prayed with such intensity and emotion that the priest, Eli, initially thought she was drunk. Hannah's prayer expressed her deep anguish, longing for a child, and her vow to dedicate her child to God if her prayer was answered.

Hannah's prayers reflected her unwavering faith and willingness to submit to God's will. Her vow to dedicate her child to God, even before knowing if she would conceive, is a testament to her trust in God's plan. Her story exemplifies the idea of surrendering one's deepest desires to the Father.

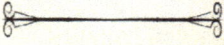

Hannah's heartfelt prayers were eventually answered. She conceived and gave birth to a son named Samuel, whose name means, "Heard by God." Her joy and gratitude are evident in her prayer of thanksgiving in 1 Samuel 2. She praised God for His faithfulness and power, illustrating her deep faith and devotion.

TESTIMONIAL

Samuel, the son born to Hannah, went on to become a significant figure in Israel's history. He became a prophet, judge, and the one who anointed both Saul and David as kings. Hannah's faith and the miracle of Samuel's birth profoundly impacted the course of Israel's history.

Hannah's story serves as a powerful testament to the emotional pain and suffering that can accompany infertility and the deep desire for children. Her unwavering faith, her willingness to submit her desires to God, and the miraculous fulfillment of her prayers inspire those facing similar challenges. It emphasizes the belief that even in the midst of sorrow, faith and persistence can lead to new moments and the realization of God's plan.

PRAYER GUIDANCE

PRAYER FOR BARNENNESS

Heavenly Father, I come before You with a heart weighed down by the burden of barrenness. I acknowledge the pain and longing I've experienced on this journey. Lord, I trust in Your plan and Your timing, even when I cannot see the way forward.

Help me find hope and healing in the midst of this challenge. May I lean on Your promises and draw strength from Your presence. Grant me the patience to wait on Your perfect timing and the faith to believe that nothing is impossible with You. I place my desires and my heart's longing, trusting that You will bring joy and transformation in Your own way, in Jesus' name.

Amen

In the space provided, offer a prayer to God, laying your feelings and desires before Him:

May this Day 8 entry offer comfort and strength to those facing the challenges of barrenness, knowing that God's plan is filled with faith and hope.

DAY 9

TITLE: <u>Building Self-Confidence</u>　　　　　**DATES:** _____

SCRIPTURE REFERENCE

2 Corinthians 12:9 (NIV)

"But he said to me, 'My grace is sufficient for you, for my power is made perfect in weakness.' Therefore, I will boast all the more gladly about my weaknesses so that Christ's power may rest on me."

SPIRITUAL THOUGHT

Today's reflection focuses on self-confidence and embracing your imperfections with faith.

SCRIPTURES OF THE DAY

Find encouragement in these verses that remind us of God's grace and power working through our imperfections:

"Therefore, do not throw away your confidence, which has a great reward.
Hebrews 10:35 (ESV)

"I praise you because I am fearfully and wonderfully made; your works are wonderful, I know that full well."
Psalm 139:14 (NIV)

GUIDED SELF-REFLECTION

Take some time to reflect on self-confidence and the idea of embracing your imperfections:

1. **Understanding Imperfections:** Reflect on the areas of your life where you've struggled with feelings of inadequacy or insecurity. What specific imperfections or weaknesses have you been trying to overcome?

----

2. **Finding God's Grace:** Consider the verse from 2 Corinthians. How can you embrace your imperfections and weaknesses as opportunities for God's grace and strength to shine through?

----

3. **Reframing Self-Image:** Think about ways to reframe your self-image by seeing yourself as God does, with love and purpose. How can this new perspective help boost your self-confidence?

TESTIMONIAL

For years, I battled with self-doubt and insecurity. It seemed like an endless cycle of negative self-talk, comparison, and seeking validation from others. I felt trapped, and the chances of getting free were slim.

Establishing a relationship with God, reading His Word, and believing what He said about me in His Word contributed greatly to my healing process. Each day, I read the pages to find scriptures that reminds me of God's unconditional love and the strength I could draw from Him. Overtime, my faith was rekindled, and with it, my self-confidence.

With this scripture as my anchor, I embarked on a journey of deliverance; I was also guided in exploring my emotions, fears, and insecurities. I realized that my lack of self-confidence was just a hurdle, not a dead-end, but I overcame it with God's grace and guidance.

Day by day, as I penned my thoughts and prayers, I felt a growing sense of empowerment. The journey was not always easy, but the scriptural wisdom and biblical testimonials gave me hope. My doubts no longer defined me; I was defined by God's promises and my confidence in Him.

TESTIMONIAL

Today, I can gladly say that I've reclaimed my self-confidence. It's not rooted in pride or arrogance but in the knowledge that I am fearfully and wonderfully made, designed for a purpose I can fulfill. I walk in faith knowing I can do all things through Christ who strengthens me (Philippians 4:19).

Self-confidence isn't just a state of mind, it's a testament to the transforming power of faith and freedom. It's a guide to rediscovering your self-confidence and stepping into the purpose God has ordained for your life; I am living proof that this journey can be yours too.

PRAYER GUIDANCE

PRAYER FOR EMOTIONAL TRAUMA

Dear God, I come before You with all my imperfections and weaknesses. Help me to see them as opportunities for Your grace and strength to shine through. Let me embrace my imperfections and boost my self-confidence through faith in Your perfect plan. As I reflect on Your Word, remind me that I am fearfully and wonderfully made and that you love me unconditionally. Fill me with confidence, not in my own abilities, but in Your power at work in me. I pray for the strength to embrace my imperfections in Jesus' name.

Amen

In the space provided, offer a prayer to God, seeking His guidance in building self-confidence by embracing your imperfections:

May this Day 9 entry guide you toward embracing your imperfections and building self-confidence through faith, knowing that God's grace is sufficient for you.

DAY 10

SCRIPTURE REFERENCE

Psalm 147:3 (AMP)

"He heals the brokenhearted and binds up their wounds [healing their pain and comforting their sorrow]."

SPIRITUAL THOUGHT

Today, as we address the wounds and trauma caused by men, let this scripture be a comforting reminder of God's capacity to mend the broken and heal the wounded.

SCRIPTURES OF THE DAY

Draw strength from these verses:

"Be kind to one another, tenderhearted, forgiving one another, as God in Christ forgave you."
Ephesians 4:32 (ESV)

"The Lord is near to the brokenhearted and saves the crushed in spirit."
Psalm 34:18 (ESV)

GUIDED SELF-REFLECTION

In addressing the wounds and trauma caused by men, consider the following reflections:

1. Identifying the Wounds: Take a moment to identify and acknowledge the emotional wounds and trauma you may carry due to past interactions with men.

----

2. Seeking Healing: Reflect on the steps you've taken or wish to take on your journey toward healing. How have your faith and God's love played a role in this process?

----

3. Forgiveness and Freedom: Contemplate the power of forgiveness in your healing journey. How can you forgive the men who caused these wounds and trauma and bring freedom and peace to your heart?

TESTIMONIAL

The story of Jacob, Leah, and their complicated relationship is an interesting narrative in the Bible, illustrating the deep wounds, pain, and emotional trauma that Leah experienced due to Jacob's lack of love for her. Jacob, the son of Isaac and Rebekah, was a central figure in the book of Genesis. He fell in love with Rachel, Leah's younger sister, and sought her hand in marriage. However, due to a trick orchestrated by their father, Laban, Jacob unknowingly marries Leah instead of Rachel.

Leah's marriage to Jacob (Genesis 29) was marked by a lack of love from him. In contrast to his deep love for Rachel, Jacob did not have the same affection for Leah. The Bible makes it clear that Leah was unloved by Jacob, which must have caused her significant emotional pain and feelings of rejection.

Leah's deep desire for Jacob's love and acceptance is evident in her actions and choices. She believed that bearing children for Jacob would win his love and affection. She named her sons with names that reflected her desire for his love, such as Reuben ("See, a son") and Simeon ("Heard by God"). She hoped that having a child would make Jacob love her each time.

Leah's actions reveal her feelings of inadequacy and the belief that she needed to prove her worth through childbearing. She seemed to try to earn Jacob's love by providing him with sons, but this only perpetuated her emotional pain and feelings of rejection.

TESTIMONIAL

Leah's sister, Rachel, also played a part in this complicated issue. Rachel's jealousy of Leah's fertility added another layer of tension and rivalry to the relationship. The competition between the two sisters further fueled the emotional turmoil within the family.

Despite Leah's difficult circumstances, and her husband's lack of love, the Bible tells us that God saw Leah's suffering and had compassion for her. He granted her children and eventually shifted her focus from seeking Jacob's love to recognizing God's love and acceptance.

The story of Jacob, Leah, and Rachel is an important reminder of the emotional pain that can result from one-sided love and rejection within a family. Leah's deep longing for acceptance and her belief that bearing children could win her husband's love illustrates the profound emotional scars she endured. Ultimately, her story also demonstrates the life-changing power of recognizing God's love and compassion, even in the midst of deep emotional wounds and rejection.

PRAYER GUIDANCE

PRAYER FOR MEN

Heavenly Father, I come before You with a heart burdened by wounds and trauma caused by men. I acknowledge the pain I've carried and the profound impact it has had on my life. Lord, I seek Your healing touch and the strength to forgive the man/men who have caused this pain. I know that I can find deliverance and peace through Your love and grace. Guide me on this journey toward wholeness, and may I find peace in Your presence. I lay down the heavy burdens I've carried for so long, trusting in Your power to heal and restore me, In Jesus' name.

Amen

In the space provided, offer a prayer to God, surrendering your wounds and trauma into His loving care:

May this Day 10 entry provide comfort and guidance as you confront the wounds and trauma caused by men, allowing God's healing love to mend your heart and bring peace to your soul.

DAY 11

SCRIPTURE REFERENCE

Isaiah 26:3 (NLT)

"You will keep in perfect peace all who trust in you, all whose thoughts are fixed on you!"

SPIRITUAL THOUGHT

As the absence of peace is addressed, let this scripture remind us of the unique peace that only God can provide, a peace that surpasses all understanding.

SCRIPTURES OF THE DAY

Receive inspiration from these verses:

"Do not be anxious about anything, but in everything by prayer and supplication with thanksgiving let your requests be made known to God. And the peace of God, which surpasses all understanding, will guard your hearts and your minds in Christ Jesus."
Philippians 4:6-7 (ESV)

"Peace I leave with you; my peace I give to you. Not as the world gives do I give to you. Let not your hearts be troubled, neither let them be afraid."
John 14:27 (ESV)

GUIDED SELF-REFLECTION

Today, explore the lack of peace in your life with the following reflections:

1. Identifying the Source: Reflect on the factors and circumstances in your life that have contributed to your lack of peace. What are the sources of your inner turmoil?

----

2. God's Gift of Peace: Contemplate the concept of God's peace, which He promises to give us. How can you align your heart and mind with His peace, especially in the midst of turmoil?

----

3. Seeking Inner Peace: Define what inner peace means to you. What steps can you take to cultivate a sense of calmness and security, even in the face of life's challenges?

TESTIMONIAL

The story of the prophet Elijah's lack of peace, and his encounter with God in 1 Kings 19, is a powerful account of a man who faced a moment of despair, inner turmoil, and exhaustion despite his boldness and faith.

Elijah was a well-known prophet in the Old Testament, celebrated for his courage and faith. However, his confrontation with the prophets of Baal, and his subsequent experience with Queen Jezebel, took a toll on him.

Elijah had just witnessed a dramatic showdown on Mount Carmel, where he challenged the prophets of the false god Baal. God demonstrated His power by sending fire to consume Elijah's sacrifice, proving He alone was the true God. After this triumph, Elijah ordered the execution of the false prophets of Baal.

Queen Jezebel, the wife of King Ahab, was a devoted worshiper of Baal and was infuriated by the death of the prophets of Baal. She sent a threatening message to Elijah, vowing to kill him within 24 hours. The gravity of this threat weighed heavily on Elijah, causing fear and a disruption of his peace.

TESTIMONIAL

Overwhelmed by Jezebel's threat, Elijah fled to the wilderness, far from Israel, in a state of hopelessness. He was physically and emotionally exhausted and he cried out to God, expressing his sense of failure and his desire to die. He had lost his sense of purpose and concentration.

In the wilderness, God reached out to Elijah. He didn't reprimand him for his despair, but provided him with food and rest. God then asked Elijah to stand on the mountain, where a powerful wind, an earthquake, and a fire passed by. However, God was not in any of these mighty displays. Instead, God revealed Himself to Elijah in a still, small voice. This gentle encounter brought Elijah the peace and assurance that he needed.

God spoke to Elijah, reaffirming his mission and appointing him to anoint future leaders and continue God's work. This reassurance, and the encounter with God, provided Elijah with a renewed sense of purpose and peace.

Elijah's story in 1 Kings 19 serves as a reminder that even the most steadfast and bold individuals can face moments of despair and inner turmoil. His encounter with God, marked by a still, small voice, showcases the importance of finding peace in God's presence, especially during times of personal and emotional crisis. It also highlights the fact that God's purpose and plan for our lives can be confirmed and renewed even in moments of deep struggle and doubt.

PRAYER GUIDANCE

PRAYER FOR NOT HAVING PEACE

Heavenly Father, I come before You with a heart burdened by the absence of peace. I acknowledge the turmoil and anxiety that have affected my well-being. Lord, I pray for the peace that only You can provide. Help me surrender my concerns and find refuge in Your loving embrace. Grant me the wisdom to keep my mind steadfast on You, even in the face of life's challenges. I seek the inner peace that can only come from You, and I trust in your divine plan for my peacefulness in Jesus' name.

Amen

In the space provided, offer a prayer to God, seeking His peace and guidance in your life:

May this Day 11 entry be a source of hope and guidance as you navigate the journey to find God's peace and healing, even in the midst of life's trials.

DAY 12

SCRIPTURE REFERENCE

Matthew 5:44 (ESV)

"But I say to you, Love your enemies and pray for those who persecute you."

SPIRITUAL THOUGHT

As we address the emotions of hate, let this scripture remind us of the power of love and forgiveness.

SCRIPTURES OF THE DAY

Find strength in these verses:

"Hatred stirs up strife, but love covers all offenses."
Proverbs 10:12 (ESV)

"Beloved, let us love one another, for love is from God, and whoever loves has been born of God and knows God."
1 John 4:7 (ESV)

GUIDED SELF-REFLECTION

Today, confront the emotions of hate with the following reflections:

1. **Identifying Hate:** Reflect on the feelings of hate you may harbor. Who or what is the object of this hate, and what has led to these emotions?

----

2. **Love and Forgiveness:** Contemplate the concept of loving your enemies and forgiving those who have wronged you. How can you release the burden of hate and embrace love and forgiveness?

----

3. **The Healing Power of Love:** Reflect on how choosing love over hate can impact your well-being and emotional healing. What steps can you take to shift from hate to love?

TESTIMONIAL

The story of Haman's hatred for the Jews, and his eventual downfall is found in the Book of Esther, one of the books of the Old Testament. It is a tale of revenge, providence, and the triumph of good over evil.

Haman was an official in the Persian Empire during the reign of King Ahasuerus (often identified with King Xerxes I). He held a high position and was extremely proud and ambitious. Haman's hatred for the Jews stemmed from a personal grudge against Mordecai, a Jewish man who worked at the king's gate.

Haman's hatred for Mordecai began when Mordecai refused to bow down to him. This refusal deeply offended Haman, and he resolved to not only seek revenge against Mordecai, but also to exterminate the entire Jewish population throughout the Persian Empire.

Haman manipulated King Ahasuerus into signing a decree that allowed the annihilation of the Jewish people on a specific date. He did this by telling the king that a group of people posed a threat to the empire and should be eliminated. The king, unaware that the decree targeted the Jews, agreed.

TESTIMONIAL

Esther, a Jewish woman who had become the queen of Persia, learned about Haman's plot. She revealed her Jewish identity to the king and pleaded for the lives of her people. King Ahasuerus was furious when he learned of the deceitful decree and asked who was responsible; Esther pointed to Haman.

King Ahasuerus ordered that Haman be hanged on the very gallows he had prepared for Mordecai. Haman's plot to annihilate the Jews was blocked, and the Jewish people were granted the right to defend themselves against their enemies. The result was a great victory for the Jews, celebrated as the holiday of Purim.

Haman's story serves as a cautionary story about the destructive power of hatred, pride, and seeking revenge. His hatred for Mordecai and the Jews led to his own downfall, demonstrating the biblical principle that those who plot harm for others may ultimately face the consequences of their own actions. The book of Esther also highlights the importance of the courage, faith, and wisdom Queen Esther displayed while facing and overcoming adversity.

PRAYER GUIDANCE

PRAYER FOR HATE

Heavenly Father, I come before You burdened by feelings of hate that have weighed heavy on my heart. I acknowledge the darkness that hate can bring into my life. God, I pray for the strength to love my enemies and forgive those who have wronged me. Help me release the burden of hate and choose the path of love and forgiveness. I seek Your healing power of love to mend my heart and bring light into the darkness. Guide me in this new beginning and help me to let go of hate in Jesus' name.

Amen

In the space provided, offer a prayer to God, laying your burdens before Him:

May this Day 12 entry be a source of inspiration and guidance
as you navigate the journey from hate to love and forgiveness,
allowing God's healing love to change your heart.

DAY 13

TITLE: <u>Sexual Immorality</u>   **DATES:**_____

SCRIPTURE REFERENCE

1 Corinthians 6:18 (NLT)

"Run from sexual sin! No other sin so clearly affects the body as this one does. For sexual immorality is a sin against your own body."

SPIRITUAL THOUGHT

As we address the issue of sexual immorality, let this scripture guide us toward understanding the sanctity of our bodies and God's call to purity.

SCRIPTURES OF THE DAY

Gain wisdom from these verses:

"Create in me a clean heart, O God, and
renew a right spirit within me."
Psalm 51:10 (ESV)

"God's will is for you to be holy, so stay away from all
sexual sin."
1 Thessalonians 4:3 (NLT)

GUIDED SELF-REFLECTION

Today, confront the issue of sexual immorality with the following reflections:

1. **Recognizing the Issue:** Reflect on any experiences or struggles related to sexual immorality (fornication, masturbation, adultery, pornography, lesbianism, sexual perversion, etc.). What has contributed to these challenges in your life?

----

2. **God's Call to Purity:** Contemplate God's call to purity and the importance of honoring your body as a temple of the Holy Spirit. How can you align your actions with God's plan for purity?

----

3. **Seeking Healing and Restoration:** Reflect on your journey toward healing and restoration from the effects of sexual immorality. What steps can you take to find forgiveness, renewal, and purity?

TESTIMONIAL

The story of the woman caught in adultery, as told in John 8:1-11 in the New Testament, is a well-known and powerful narrative that illustrates the compassion and wisdom of Jesus when faced with a moral dilemma. In this story, a group of scribes and Pharisees brought a woman who had been caught in the act of adultery before Jesus. They sought to use her as a trap to challenge Jesus' authority and teachings.

The Scribes and Pharisees presented the woman and reminded Jesus that the Mosaic Law prescribed stoning as the punishment for adultery. They asked Him what should be done with her, seemingly forcing Him to either uphold the law and condemn the woman or disregard the law and appear to go against the religious traditions. Instead of giving a direct answer, Jesus bent down and began writing on the ground with His finger.

Although it is unknown what He wrote, it is often interpreted as Jesus' way of reflecting and perhaps reminding the accusers of their sins.

When the Scribes and Pharisees continued to press Him for an answer, Jesus responded with a challenge: "Let him who is without sin among you be the first to throw a stone at her." This response called for contemplation and self-examination, highlighting the idea that none of them were free from sin. One by one, beginning with the eldest, the accusers began to leave, realizing their own imperfections. In the end, only Jesus and the woman remained.

TESTIMONIAL

Jesus then asked the woman where her accusers had gone and if anyone had condemned her; she replied that no one had. Jesus, displaying compassion and mercy, told her, "Neither do I condemn you. Go, and from now on, sin no more." His words extended forgiveness to the woman and encouraged her to change her ways.

⚬────────⚬

This story is often cited as a powerful example of Jesus' emphasis on mercy, forgiveness, and the idea that no one is without sin. It challenges the accusers to reflect on their own imperfections and serves as a reminder of the importance of compassion and understanding in matters of judgment and justice.

PRAYER GUIDANCE

PRAYER FOR SEXUAL IMMORALITY

Heavenly Father, I come before You, acknowledging the struggles and challenges I have faced regarding sexual immorality. I recognize the importance of purity and the sanctity of my body. Lord, I seek Your forgiveness and healing. Create in me a clean heart and renew a right spirit within me. Help me break free from the chains of sexual immorality and lead me to purity. I place my trust in Your supernatural power and seek the strength to honor my body as a temple of the Holy Spirit in Jesus' name.

Amen

In the space provided, offer a prayer to God, seeking His forgiveness, healing, and guidance in your journey towards purity:

May this Day 13 entry provide you with hope and guidance as you navigate the journey toward purity, forgiveness, and healing, allowing God's grace to mend your heart and deliver you from sexual immorality.

DAY 14

TITLE: <u>Jealousy</u>   **DATES:** _____

SCRIPTURE REFERENCE

James 3:16 (ESV)

Scripture of the Day: "For where jealousy and selfish ambition exist, there will be disorder and every vile practice."

SPIRITUAL THOUGHT

As the issue of jealousy is being addressed, let this scripture guide us towards understanding the destructive nature of jealousy and the importance of establishing a heart of contentment.

SCRIPTURES OF THE DAY

Draw wisdom from these verses:

"Keep your life free from love of money, and be content with what you have, for he has said, 'I will never leave you nor forsake you.'"
Hebrews 13:5 (ESV)

"Let your character be free from the love of money, being content with what you have; for He Himself has said, 'I will never desert you, nor will I ever forsake you.'"
Hebrews 13:5 (NASB)

GUIDED SELF-REFLECTION

Today, confront the issue of jealousy with the following reflections:

1. **Identifying Jealousy:** Reflect on moments or situations where you have experienced jealousy. What were the triggers, and how did it affect your well-being?

----

2. **The Destructive Nature of Jealousy:** Contemplate the harmful effects of jealousy on your emotional and spiritual life. How does jealousy contribute to disorder and conflict?

----

3. **Cultivating Contentment:** Reflect on the concept of contentment and how it can counterattack jealousy. What steps can you take to nurture a heart of gratitude and satisfaction?

TESTIMONIAL

The story of Hagar and Sarah's jealousy and mistreatment is found in the book of Genesis 16 and 21. Hagar was Sarah's Egyptian maidservant, and the two women were involved in a complex and challenging situation.

At that particular moment, Sarah, the wife of Abraham, was unable to have children, and she was desperate to fulfill God's promise of descendants. She decided to take matters into her own hands by giving her maidservant, Hagar, to Abraham as a secondary wife, hoping that Hagar would bear a child in her place.

Hagar became pregnant with Abraham's child, Ishmael, and her pregnancy created tensions and jealousy between her and Sarah. Sarah felt mistreated, likely because Hagar's pregnancy gave her a sense of superiority and vindication, which led to conflict and mistreatment between the two women. The situation became so unbearable for Hagar that she fled into the wilderness to escape Sarah's mistreatment. Pregnant and alone, Hagar found herself in a desperate and vulnerable situation.

TESTIMONIAL

In the wilderness, Hagar had a profound encounter with God. The Bible tells us that the Angel of the Lord found her by a spring of water. God reassured Hagar, promising that her descendants would be numerous, and that she should return to Sarah's household. Hagar recognized this encounter as an encounter with God and called Him "the God who sees." She returned and gave birth to Ishmael.

This story accounts for the struggles and complexities of human relationships, including jealousy and mistreatment. It also highlights God's compassion and guidance in times of distress. Hagar's encounter with God in the wilderness, and her recognition that God sees and cares for her, demonstrate an example of divine intervention and care for the dismissed and defeated. The story of Hagar and Sarah serves as a reminder of the importance of understanding our interactions with others and the reassuring presence of God in our times of need.

PRAYER GUIDANCE

PRAYER FOR JEALOUSY

God, I come before You acknowledging the presence of jealousy in my heart. I recognize the harm it can cause and the importance of contentment. Father, I pray for Your guidance and strength to overcome jealousy. Help me to nurture a heart of gratitude and satisfaction, free from the destructive nature of jealousy. I seek Your help to release jealousy and embrace contentment in Jesus' name.

Amen

In the space provided, offer a prayer to God, seeking His guidance in overcoming jealousy and cultivating a heart of contentment:

May this Day 14 entry provide you with hope and guidance as you navigate the journey toward contentment, releasing the grip of jealousy and finding healing through faith.

DAY 15

TITLE: <u>Envy</u>   **DATES:**_____

SCRIPTURE REFERENCE

Galatians 5:26 (ESV)

"Let us not become conceited, provoking one another, envying one another."

SPIRITUAL THOUGHT

As we address the issue of envy, let this scripture guide us toward understanding the harmful effects of envy on our relationships and the importance of humility.

SCRIPTURES OF THE DAY

Gain another level of wisdom and understanding from these verses:

"Do nothing from rivalry or conceit, but in humility count others more significant than yourselves."
Philippians 2:3 (ESV)

"But if you have bitter jealousy and selfish ambition in your hearts, do not boast and be false to the truth."
James 3:14 (ESV)

GUIDED SELF-REFLECTION

Today, confront the issue of envy with the following reflections:

1. **Recognizing Envy**: Reflect on moments or situations where you have experienced envy. What were the triggers, and how did it affect your relationships and inner peace?

----

2. **The Destructive Nature of Envy**: Contemplate the harmful effects of envy on your emotional and spiritual life. How does envy lead to conflict and discontentment?

----

3. **Cultivating Humility**: Reflect on the concept of humility and how it can destroy envy. What steps can you take to nurture a humble heart and celebrate the blessings of others?

TESTIMONIAL

The story of King Ahab, Queen Jezebel, and their envy of Naboth's vineyard is found in 1 Kings 21. It serves as a warning about the consequences of greed and the abuse of power.

Naboth, an Israelite, owned a vineyard located near the palace of King Ahab in the city of Jezreel. Ahab desired Naboth's vineyard, as it was well-located and suitable for a garden. King Ahab approached Naboth, asking him to sell the vineyard or exchange it for a better one. However, Naboth refused, explaining that it was an inheritance from his family and that he could not sell it.

When King Ahab returned home and expressed his disappointment over Naboth's refusal, Queen Jezebel devised a cunning plan to obtain the vineyard for her husband. She sent letters in Ahab's name to the elders and nobles of Jezreel, instructing them to arrange for a false trial in which Naboth would be falsely accused of blasphemy and stoned to death.

TESTIMONIAL

The elders and nobles followed Jezebel's orders, and Naboth was falsely accused and stoned to death. With Naboth dead, Ahab took possession of the vineyard. God sent the prophet Elijah to confront Ahab with a message of judgment. Elijah prophesied that Ahab's dynasty would be cut off and that both Ahab and Jezebel would meet tragic ends as punishment for their wickedness.

This story serves as a powerful cautionary tale about the consequences of greed, manipulation, and abuse of power. It illustrates the corrupting influence of envy and the lengths to which people may go to satisfy their desires. It also underscores the idea that God's justice will ultimately prevail, and those who engage in wrongdoing will face God's judgment.

PRAYER GUIDANCE

PRAYER FOR ENVY

Father, I come before You, acknowledging the presence of envy in my heart. I recognize the harm it can cause and the importance of humility. Lord, I pray for Your guidance and strength to overcome envy. Help me to nurture a humble heart and celebrate the blessings of others, free from the destructive nature of envy. I seek Your strength to release envy and embrace humility in Jesus' name.

Amen

In the space provided, offer a prayer to God, seeking His guidance in overcoming envy and cultivating a humble heart:

May this Day 15 entry provide you with hope and guidance as you navigate the journey towards humility, releasing the grip of envy, and finding healing through faith.

DAY 16

TITLE: <u>Competition</u>   **DATES:**_____

SCRIPTURE REFERENCE

Genesis 30:1 (BSB)

"When Rachel saw that she was not bearing any children for Jacob, she envied her sister. "Give me children, or I will die!" she said to Jacob.

SPIRITUAL THOUGHT

As we move into the topic of competition, this scripture encourages us to approach it with humility and a mindset of esteeming others more highly than ourselves.

SCRIPTURES OF THE DAY

Draw wisdom from these verses:

"But if you have bitter jealousy and selfish ambition in your hearts, do not boast and be false to the truth."
James 3:14 (ESV)

"Pay careful attention to your own work, for then you will get the satisfaction of a job well done, and you won't need to compare yourself to anyone else."
Galatians 6:4 (NLT)

GUIDED SELF-REFLECTION

Today's self-reflection is about understanding competition and its effects:

1. **Competition in Your Life:** Reflect on situations where you have experienced competition. It could be in your personal, professional, or social life. What were the triggers for these competitive feelings?

----

2. **The Impact of Competition:** Consider how competition has influenced your emotions, relationships, and self-esteem. Has it led to negative feelings or behaviors?

----

3. **Embracing Humility:** Contemplate how you can adopt a humble approach to competition. How can you shift your focus from winning to building positive relationships and personal growth?

TESTIMONIAL

The story of Rachel's competition with her sister Leah over their husband Jacob's affections, and the matter of bearing children, is found in the book of Genesis, primarily in chapters 29 and 30. It presents a difficult and emotionally charged family issue.

Jacob fell deeply in love with Rachel, the youngest daughter of Laban. He worked for Laban for seven years to earn Rachel's hand in marriage. However, Laban played a trick on Jacob by substituting Rachel with her older sister, Leah, on their wedding night. Jacob, unaware of the deception, consummated his marriage with Leah. After their marriage, Leah began conceiving children for Jacob, while Rachel remained barren. Leah gave birth to several sons, including Reuben, Simeon, Levi, and Judah. Her fertility was a source of competition and jealousy between the sisters.

Rachel was envious of her sister's ability to bear children for Jacob and longed for her own children. She pleaded with Jacob for children and even took the unconventional step of offering her maidservant, Bilhah, to Jacob as a concubine to bear children on her behalf. Bilhah bore two sons for Rachel.

TESTIMONIAL

Not to be outdone, Leah also entered into the competition by giving her maidservant, Zilpah, to Jacob as a concubine, resulting in the birth of two more sons. This rivalry persisted as each sister tried to secure Jacob's affection and build up her own legacy through childbearing. Eventually, God heard Rachel's plea and allowed her to conceive. She gave birth to Joseph and later to Benjamin.

———

This story serves as an intense depiction of the complications of human relationships, particularly within a family, where sibling rivalry and jealousy can arise from unmet desires. It highlights the emotional pain and longing resulting from unfulfilled expectations, such as the desire for children. God eventually allowed Rachel to conceive and have children, emphasizing the importance of patience, faith, and God's role in fulfilling promises and desires.

PRAYER GUIDANCE

PRAYER FOR COMPETITION

God, I come before You with a heart burdened by the competitive nature of this world. I acknowledge the negative impact it can have on my emotions and relationships. Lord, I pray for Your guidance to help me approach competition with humility.

May I focus on building genuine relationships and personal growth rather than striving solely for victory. I seek the power and authority of Jesus to release the grip of competition and embrace humility and love in Jesus' name.

Amen

In the space provided, offer a prayer to God, seeking His guidance in approaching competition with humility and love.

May this Day 16 entry provide you with guidance and expectation as you navigate the difficult emotions surrounding competition, seeking unity and personal growth through faith.

DAY 17

TITLE: <u>The Power of Transparency</u>   DATES:_____

SCRIPTURE REFERENCE

1 John 1:7 (ESV)

"But if we walk in the light, as he is in the light, we have fellowship with one another, and the blood of Jesus his Son cleanses us from all sin."

SPIRITUAL THOUGHT

Today's reflection centers on the importance of transparency and walking in the light of God's truth.

SCRIPTURES OF THE DAY

Draw wisdom and hope from these verses that emphasize the importance of transparency in our faith journey:

"Then you will know the truth, and the truth will set you free."
John 8:32 (NIV)

"Whoever conceals his transgressions will not prosper, but he who confesses and forsakes them will obtain mercy."
Proverbs 28:13 (ESV)

GUIDED SELF-REFLECTION

Take some time to reflect on transparency and the role it plays in your healing journey:

1. **Understanding Transparency**: What does transparency mean to you? Consider how being open and honest can bring healing to your life and relationships.

----

2. **Recognizing Barriers**: Reflect on any barriers or fears that have prevented you from being transparent in the past. What is holding you back from fully embracing transparency?

----

3. **The Power of God's Light**: How can walking in the light, as mentioned in 1 John 1:7, bring healing and freedom into your life? In what ways can God's truth and love dispel darkness and secrecy?

TESTIMONIAL

During my own journey towards healing and restoration, I have had the privilege of connecting with incredible women, each of whom carries a unique story of pain, transformation, and purpose. In "You Have No Idea the Hell I've Been Through 22: Women Who Pushed from Pain to Purpose," I had the privilege of being featured alongside 21 other incredible women. We shared our raw and authentic testimonies, shedding light on the profound pain we endured, and how it served as a catalyst for finding our true purpose.

Transparency is a deep strength parallel to the truth supporting our faith. The stories shared in this anthology reveal the depths of my own trials. In this anthology, I talked about how I grew up witnessing my father abuse my mother, a heartbreaking experience that shaped my early life. As a child, I also endured being sexually abused by a family member, a burden that I carried into my adulthood. To compound the weight of these trials, I faced racial and sexual discrimination, a painful ordeal that resulted in being blackballed from the military.

But here's the amazing part: where the light begins seeping into the cracks of misery. Through transparency, and the act of revealing our pain and brokenness, we found our strength. These experiences, often the greatest trials we face, became the stepping stones to our purposes. Transparency was the key that unlocked the healing in our lives.

TESTIMONIAL

It was in our willingness to share our pain, vulnerability, and faith that we discovered the incredible strength found in unity. The stories within this anthology showcase the beauty that emerges from brokenness and the powerful purpose that can arise from life's most challenging moments.

I hope that by sharing my experiences, and joining hands with these courageous women, we can collectively inspire and uplift others on their paths to healing and restoration. Transparency isn't just about revealing our past. It's about God shining His light on the incredible potential that lies in our future. May the journey of transparency and healing continue to guide us toward the purpose God has in store for us.

This anthology was pivotal in allowing us, as authors, to open up and heal. It allowed us to turn our past pain into purpose, giving voice to our experiences and inspiring others to overcome their own challenges.

In addition to my anthology, I've also authored "What's Blocking Your Confidence? Effective Ways to Conquer Your Fears (Second Edition)." Because the enemy seeks to use fear as a weapon to hinder us from receiving the confidence that God has destined for us, I wanted the reader to know that this book explores the profound impact of fear in our lives and how it can be a powerful weapon used against us.

TESTIMONIAL

Through faith and a deep understanding of God's truth, I shared how we can conquer these fears and step boldly into the life that He has uniquely designed for us to have so that we can boldly step into the purpose.

The stories shared, and the wisdom imparted in these books, offer hope to all women who may be wrestling with their own pain, self-doubt, and/or insecurities. They do not just showcase transparency.

They also actively promote healing, encouragement, and personal growth. It is my mission to equip others with the tools and knowledge to break free from the chains of insecurity and step boldly onto the path that God has laid before them. Through the transparency of these stories, I hope to impart the truth of our experiences and the power of resilience, faith, and the unwavering belief that, like us, others can push through pain. They can emerge stronger, walking in the confidence God ordained for their lives.

Together, we can find healing, purpose, and the courage to face any trial, for the truth we share has the power to set us free. Transparency is the bridge from pain to purpose, and by sharing our stories, we walk along the path toward the healing and redemption that God has promised us.

PRAYER GUIDANCE

PRAYER FOR THE POWER OF TRANSPARENCY

Heavenly Father, I come before You with a desire to walk in the light of Your truth. Help me overcome my fears and barriers to transparency. Guide me in being open, honest, and vulnerable in my relationships and with You. Lord, I recognize that true healing comes through honesty and confession. As I reflect on Your Word, and the examples of others, show me how to embrace transparency as a means to healing and freedom. I pray for the courage to walk in the truth in Jesus' name.

Amen

In the space provided, offer a prayer to God, seeking His guidance in cultivating transparency:

May this Day 17 entry inspire you to receive your transparency as a path to healing and a deeper connection with God and others.

DAY 18

TITLE: <u>Abuse</u>   **DATES:_____**

SCRIPTURE REFERENCE

Psalm 30:2 (NIV)

"LORD my God, I called to you for help, and you healed me."

SPIRITUAL THOUGHT

As we address the topic of abuse, let this scripture remind us that God is our refuge and stronghold during difficult times.

SCRIPTURES OF THE DAY

Find comfort and strength in these verses:

"The Lord is close to the brokenhearted and saves those who are crushed in spirit."
Psalm 34:18 (NIV)

"He heals the brokenhearted and binds up their wounds."
Psalm 147:3 (NIV)

GUIDED SELF-REFLECTION

Today's self-reflection is about recognizing and healing from the effects of abuse:

1. Acknowledging the Pain: Take a moment to acknowledge the pain and trauma that may have resulted from abuse (physical, verbal, sexual, etc.) in your life. Write down your feelings and experiences.

----

2. The Impact on Your Well-being: Reflect on how abuse has affected your emotional, physical, and mental well-being. What challenges have you faced as a result?

----

3. Steps Towards Healing: Consider what steps you can take to heal from the effects of abuse. How can your faith and support systems assist in this process?

TESTIMONIAL

The biblical story of Tamar, the daughter of King David, is a tragic and disturbing narrative found specifically in 2 Samuel 13.

Tamar was the beautiful daughter of King David and Maacah, and her half-brother Amnon, the son of David and Ahinoam, developed an intense and unhealthy infatuation with her. Amnon's feelings for Tamar grew into an obsession, which led him to a dark and sinful plan to be alone with her.

Amnon faked being sick and requested that Tamar come to his quarters to prepare food for him, as it was customary for family members to care for one another. Being an obedient and caring sister, Tamar went to tend to him, unaware of Amnon's true intentions.

When Tamar arrived, Amnon took advantage of her trust and vulnerability. He forced her into a room and raped her, committing a grave sin and violating her in the most horrifying way possible. After the assault, Amnon's feelings for Tamar turned to hate and disgust, and he cold heartedly dismissed her. Tamar left in a state of shock, humiliation, and despair, tore her clothes, and put ashes on her head, which is a traditional sign of mourning.

TESTIMONIAL

Tamar's full brother, Absalom, learned of the terrible crime committed against his sister. Filled with a burning desire for revenge and justice, he bided his time. Absalom organized a feast two years later and invited all of David's sons, including Amnon. During the feast, with the intent to avenge his sister's honor, Absalom ordered his servants to kill Amnon. They carried out this act, resulting in Amnon's death.

Tamar, Amnon, and Absalom's story is a heartbreaking example of the devastating consequences of unchecked lust, betrayal, and vengeance within a family. It also highlights the importance of seeking justice and support for victims of abuse and assault. These events had far-reaching consequences for King David's family, leading to strife and division within the kingdom and illustrating the far-reaching impact of such tragic incidents.

PRAYER GUIDANCE

PRAYER FOR ABUSE

Heavenly Father, I come before You with a heavy heart, acknowledging the pain and trauma of abuse in my life. I lay my burdens at Your feet and seek Your refuge. Lord, I ask for Your healing touch to mend the wounds and brokenness caused by abuse. May Your strength and love provide comfort and restoration. Guide me on the path to healing and help me find the support I need. I surrender these burdens, trusting in Your divine plan for my restoration in Jesus' name.

Amen

In the space provided, offer a prayer to God, seeking His guidance and healing from the effects of abuse.

May this Day 18 entry offer you a source of strength and healing as you confront the painful effects of abuse with faith and restoration.

DAY 19

TITLE: <u>Telling Lies</u>   **DATES:**_____

SCRIPTURE REFERENCE

Proverbs 12:22 (NIV)

"The Lord detests lying lips, but he delights in people who are trustworthy."

SPIRITUAL THOUGHT

As we go into the topic of telling lies, remember that honesty and trustworthiness are values cherished by God.

SCRIPTURES OF THE DAY

Draw wisdom and inspiration from these verses:

"Therefore, each of you must put off falsehood and speak truthfully to your neighbor, for we are all members of one body."
Ephesians 4:25 (NIV)

"Do not lie to one another, seeing that you have put off the old self with its practices and have put on the new self, which is being renewed in knowledge after the image of its creator."
Colossians 3:9-10 (ESV)

GUIDED SELF-REFLECTION

Today, engage in self-reflection regarding the issue of telling lies:

1. Acknowledging the Deception: Take a moment to reflect on times you have been untruthful. What motivated you to tell lies, and what were the consequences?

----

2. Impact on Relationships: Consider how lying may have affected your relationships, trust, and your own sense of integrity. Write down your thoughts and emotions.

----

3. The Path to Honesty: Think about the steps you can take to embrace honesty and restore trust in your relationships. How can your faith guide you in this journey?

TESTIMONIAL

The story of Ananias and Sapphira is found in Acts 5:1-11. It is a story of deceit and the consequences of lying.

Ananias and Sapphira were early followers of Jesus Christ who lived in Jerusalem. They sold a piece of property and decided to bring a portion of the proceeds to the apostles to contribute to the community's needs. However, they conspired to withhold a part of the money while pretending to present the entire sum.

Ananias presented the money to the apostles but claimed that the amount he gave was the full proceeds from the sale of the property. He lied about the actual amount, trying to deceive the apostles and the community. The apostle Peter, filled with the Holy Spirit, discerned the deceit and confronted Ananias. He accused Ananias of lying not to men, but to God. Peter made it clear that Ananias had full control over the money and was not obligated to give it all. Upon hearing Peter's rebuke, Ananias fell to the ground and died instantly, resulting in his sudden death striking fear into those who witnessed it.

TESTIMONIAL

After the death of her husband, Sapphira arrived, not knowing what had happened. Peter questioned her about the amount they had received for the property, and she confirmed the false amount that Ananias had given. Like her husband, Sapphira was also rebuked and confronted with her lie. She, too, fell down dead, and she was buried beside her husband.

 The story of Ananias and Sapphira serves as a striking illustration of the seriousness of deceit and hypocrisy. It emphasizes the importance of honesty and integrity, especially in matters of faith and community. Their sudden deaths were seen as a divine judgment and a powerful lesson, underlining the principle that God values truth and sincerity and that dishonesty can have severe consequences.

PRAYER GUIDANCE

PRAYER FOR TELLING LIES

Heavenly Father, I come before You with a humble heart, acknowledging the times I have been untruthful. I ask for Your forgiveness and guidance. God, help me to embrace honesty and truthfulness in my words and actions. Grant me the wisdom to restore trust in my relationships and the strength to overcome the urge to lie. May my faith in You be a source of strength and integrity. I seek to walk the path of truth in Jesus' name.

Amen

In the space provided, offer a prayer to God, seeking His guidance and the strength to be truthful:

May this Day 19 entry be a step towards healing and embracing honesty in your life, guided by faith and the desire to build trust in your relationships.

DAY 20
TITLE: <u>Embracing Your Body Image</u>   **DATES:**_____

SCRIPTURE REFERENCE

Psalm 139:14 (NIV)

"I praise you because I am fearfully and wonderfully made; your works are wonderful, I know that full well."

SPIRITUAL THOUGHT

Today, let's dive into the journey of embracing your body image and recognizing the beauty in God's creation.

SCRIPTURES OF THE DAY

Let these verses remind you of the beauty of God's creation and the importance of self-acceptance:

"But the LORD said to Samuel, "Do not consider his appearance or height, for I have rejected him. The LORD does not look at the things people look at. People look at the outward appearance, but the LORD looks at the heart."
1 Samuel 16:7 (NIV)

"Do you not know that your bodies are temples of the Holy Spirit, who is in you, whom you have received from God? You are not your own."
1 Corinthians 6:19 (NIV)

GUIDED SELF-REFLECTION

Reflect on your relationship with your body image:

1. **Your Body as God's Creation:** Consider how you view your body as a creation of God. How has your perception of your body image evolved during your healing journey? Write down your thoughts.

----

2. **Challenges and Triumphs:** Reflect on the challenges and triumphs you've experienced related to body image. What moments of self-acceptance have you had, and what struggles remain? Share your experiences.

----

3. **God's Perspective:** Imagine how God sees you. How does His unconditional love and acceptance influence how you perceive your own body? Write about your understanding of your body from a faith-based perspective.

TESTIMONIAL

There were times in my life when I carried the heavy burden of body image insecurities. The constant comparison to unrealistic beauty standards and the pursuit of so-called perfection left me feeling inadequate and, at times, deeply unhappy with my own reflection. It seemed like a never-ending battle, and the chase for an ideal that constantly escaped me, took a toll on my mental and emotional well-being.

But somewhere along the way, a change began to take place within me, a journey that led me to the realization – the imperfections that I once despised were, in fact, the very essence of my uniqueness and beauty.

This revelation did not happen overnight, it was a process of self-discovery and self-acceptance. I started by challenging the negative thoughts that had bothered me for so long. I began to question why I was so hard on myself and placed so much importance on superficial appearance. I realized that the never-ending quest for an idealized version of myself was not only unattainable, but also detrimental to my mental and emotional health.

As I shifted my perspective, I began to see beauty in what I thought were imperfections that had once tormented me. I started to understand that the scars and flaws on my body were a part of my unique story. They were the marks of the experiences that had shaped me, a testament to the battles I had fought, and the triumphs I had achieved. They were not blemishes, they were marks of resilience.

TESTIMONIAL

Embracing imperfections meant embracing my true self. It was a powerful act of self-love that allowed me to break free from the suffocating confines of society's beauty ideals. I found freedom in accepting my body as it was and all its imperfections. This freedom was powerful and allowed me to redirect my focus toward what truly mattered – my inner worth, character, and the impact I could make in the world with God's help.

I started to see the beauty in others' imperfections as well, realizing that we are all wonderfully flawed and that these imperfections are what makes us human. My relationships improved as I let go of judgment and comparison, allowing me to connect with people on a deeper level.

Embracing imperfections has been a journey towards self-love and self-acceptance. It has taught me that beauty is not defined by external appearances, but by the kindness in one's heart, the depth of one's character, and the love we share with others.

Today, I stand before you as someone who has embraced their imperfections and, in doing so, found a profound and lasting sense of self-worth and self-love. I encourage anyone struggling with body image insecurities to embark on this journey of loving and accepting yourself as you are because the beauty of embracing imperfections is nothing short of life-changing.

PRAYER GUIDANCE

PRAYER FOR EMBRACING YOUR BODY IMAGE

Heavenly Father, I come before You with gratitude for the body You've fearfully and wonderfully made. Help me, Lord, to see myself as You see me, with love and acceptance. Guide me as I continue to heal and embrace my body image. Give me strength in moments of self-doubt and grace in moments of self-acceptance. May I find peace knowing I am Your beautifully and wonderfully made creation. I pray for a loving perspective on my body image in Jesus' name.

Amen

In the space provided, offer a prayer to God, thanking Him for your body and asking for guidance in embracing your body image:

May this Day 20 entry inspire you to embrace your body image with the knowledge that you are wonderfully made in God's image.

DAY 21

TITLE: <u>Learning to Say "No"</u>   **DATES:**_____

SCRIPTURE REFERENCE

Matthew 5:37 (NKJV)

"But let your 'Yes' be 'Yes,' and your 'No,' 'No.' For whatever is more than these is from the evil one."

SPIRITUAL THOUGHT

As we continue your healing journey, today focuses on setting healthy boundaries and learning to say no.

SCRIPTURES OF THE DAY

Find strength in these verses, which emphasize the importance of clear and honest communication:

"Don't visit your neighbors too often, or you will wear out your welcome.
Proverbs 25:17 (NLT)

"Above all, my brothers and sisters, do not swear–not by heaven, earth, or anything else. You only need to say a simple 'Yes' or 'No.' Otherwise, you will be condemned."
James 5:12 (NIV)

GUIDED SELF-REFLECTION

**Reflect on your understanding and practice of
setting boundaries and saying (No):**

1. **Defining Personal Boundaries:** What personal boundaries
have you established, or need to establish, for your well-being
and healing journey? Write down the boundaries that come to
mind.

----------.---
----

2. **Challenges and Triumphs:** Share your experiences of setting
boundaries and saying (No). What challenges have you faced,
and what triumphs have you achieved? Reflect on the impact
these experiences have had on your healing process.

----

3. **Faith-Based Decision Making:** Consider how your faith
influences your ability to set boundaries and say (No). How does
the Scripture for today guide you in making these decisions?
Write about your faith-based approach to boundaries.

TESTIMONIAL

Throughout my life, I've struggled with the fear of disappointing others, not meeting their expectations, being nice and going along when things would offend me and make me uncomfortable, and the persistent need to be a continual "yes-woman." These self-imposed limitations left me emotionally drained, overwhelmed, and often disconnected from my own needs and desires.

This is a gentle yet powerful reminder that setting boundaries is an act of self-love. It's not about building walls, but creating space to nurture our well-being, dreams, and spiritual growth.

The Father has given me has given me the wisdom and courage to say "No" when needed. The assurance of God's love and grace strengthens my spirit, assuring me that my self-worth isn't contingent on the opinions of others.

In learning to set boundaries, I have discovered freedom. I am no longer a prisoner of others' expectations. I can devote my time and energy to what truly matters–nurturing my relationship with God, my well-being, and the people and passions developing my life.

TESTIMONIAL

Setting clear and necessary boundaries has led me in a direction where I can explore my emotions, seek God's guidance, and find peace in His love. It's not simply a choice, it's a lifestyle on the journey to becoming the woman God created me to be because learning to say "No" is needed for growth, restoration, and the development of faith-filled boundaries.

As I reflect on this journey of exploring boundaries and learning to say "No," I am reminded that this process is ongoing, guided by faith, freedom, and the strength to protect my well-being. This journal entry has been a vital moment of fulfillment, confirming that I have the power to set boundaries, protect my peace, and nurture my spirit. I carry this wisdom in my heart, knowing that with God's grace, I can face the world with confidence, compassion, and an unwavering commitment to my own well-being.

The journey continues, and I am ready to embrace it with open arms, knowing that I am on the path to becoming the woman I am meant to be.

PRAYER GUIDANCE

PRAYER FOR SETTING BOUNDARIES

Dear Heavenly Father, I come before You, recognizing the importance of setting healthy boundaries and being honest in my "Yes" and "No." Grant me the wisdom to establish boundaries that protect my well-being and honor You. Give me the strength to say "No" when necessary and the grace to do so with love and respect. Guide me in making decisions that align with Your will. May my faith be the foundation of my actions, and I find peace in the boundaries I set. I request Your guidance on this aspect of my healing journey in Jesus' name.

Amen

In the space provided, offer a prayer to God, seeking His guidance and strength in setting boundaries and learning to say (No):

May this Day 21 entry inspire you to set boundaries and learn to say no when it serves your well-being and aligns with God's will.

DAY 22

TITLE: <u>What Is Your Purpose?</u>   **DATES:**_____

SCRIPTURE REFERENCE

Jeremiah 29:11 (NIV)

"For I know the plans I have for you," declares the LORD, "plans to prosper you and not to harm you, plans to give you hope and a future."

SPIRITUAL THOUGHT

In our journey of healing, it's essential to explore God's purpose for us.

SCRIPTURES OF THE DAY

Find inspiration in these verses:

"But you are a chosen race, a royal priesthood, a holy nation, a people for his own possession, that you may proclaim the excellencies of him who called you out of darkness into his marvelous light."
1 Peter 2:9 (ESV)

"Commit your work to the Lord, and your plans will be established."
Proverbs 16:3 (ESV)

GUIDED SELF-REFLECTION

Today, engage in self-reflection on the topic of your purpose:

1. **Exploring Your Calling:** Take time to reflect on your life's purpose. What do you feel called to do, whether it's related to your career, relationships, or a particular mission?

----

2. **Barriers to Fulfillment:** Consider any barriers or obstacles that have prevented you from fully embracing your purpose. Write down your thoughts and emotions.

----

3. **Embracing God's Plan:** How can your faith guide you in discovering and embracing God's plan for your life? What steps can you take to align your purpose with His divine will?

TESTIMONIAL

Samuel's purpose is clearly revealed, particularly in the Book of 1 Samuel. Samuel was born to a woman named Hannah, who had been barren and prayed fervently to God for a son. In her desperation, she made a vow to dedicate her son to the service of God if she were granted a child. God heard her prayers, and Samuel was born. After he was weaned, Hannah fulfilled her vow, and she brought Samuel to the tabernacle at Shiloh, where the high priest Eli was serving.

Samuel's purpose became evident as he grew. He served in the house of the Lord under Eli's guidance. One night, Samuel was resting in the temple and heard a voice calling his name. He assumed it was Eli, but after several such incidents, Eli realized that the Lord was calling Samuel. Eli instructed Samuel to respond, "Speak, Lord, for your servant is listening." When Samuel did so, God spoke to him and revealed His plans.

God's purpose for Samuel was to become a prophet and a judge in Israel. He was chosen to deliver God's messages to the people, guide them in their affairs, and anoint the first two kings of Israel, Saul and David. Samuel faithfully fulfilled his role as a prophet and a judge, playing a crucial part in the transition from the period of the judges to the establishment of a monarchy in Israel.

TESTIMONIAL

The story of Samuel's calling and his fulfillment of God's purpose emphasizes the idea that God has a plan for each individual, and sometimes that purpose is revealed through direct communication with Him.

Samuel's life serves as an example of someone who recognized and embraced his divine calling and played a significant role in the history of Israel.

PRAYER GUIDANCE

PRAYER FOR WHAT IS YOUR PURPOSE

Father, I come before You, yearning to understand Your purpose for my life. Help me to discover the calling You have placed in my heart. Guide me in overcoming any barriers that stand in the way of fulfilling that purpose. May I find strength and healing as I align my life with Your divine plan. Lord, grant me the wisdom to discern Your will and the courage to walk in the path You have set before me. I seek to live a life of purpose and meaningful, in Jesus' name.

Amen

In the space provided, offer a prayer to God, seeking His guidance in understanding and fulfilling your purpose:

May this Day 22 entry be a step toward understanding and embracing God's purpose for your life, guided by faith and the desire to fulfill His plan.

DAY 23

TITLE: <u>What Is Your Gift?</u>   **DATES:_____**

SCRIPTURE REFERENCE

1 Peter 4:10 (ESV)

"As each has received a gift, use it to serve one another as good stewards of God's varied grace."

SPIRITUAL THOUGHT

Your gifts are a source of healing and blessing. Women have harnessed their God-given talents to overcome challenges and find their purpose. Today, let us explore the unique gifts God has bestowed upon each of us.

SCRIPTURES OF THE DAY

Find encouragement in these verses:

"For we are his workmanship, created in Christ Jesus for good works, which God prepared beforehand, that we should walk in them."
Ephesians 2:10 (ESV)

"Every good gift and every perfect gift is from above, coming down from the Father of lights, with whom there is no variation or shadow due to change."
James 1:17 (ESV)

GUIDED SELF-REFLECTION

Engage in self-reflection regarding your God-given gifts:

1. **Identifying Your Gifts:** Take a moment to consider your talents and abilities. What are you naturally gifted at? Write them down.

----

2. **Purpose in Your Gifts:** How can your gifts be used to serve others or fulfill your life's purpose? Explore how your talents can be a source of healing for yourself and others.

----

3. **Overcoming Doubt:** Sometimes, we doubt our own abilities. Reflect on any doubts or insecurities you may have about your gifts and consider how faith can help overcome them.

TESTIMONIAL

The Bible contains various stories of individuals discovering and using their God-given gifts and talents. One notable story is that of David, who discovered his gift and calling when he was anointed by the prophet Samuel.

David's story can be found in 1 Samuel 16. At the time, Saul was the reigning king of Israel, but God had rejected him as king due to his disobedience. God instructed the prophet Samuel to anoint a new king from the house of Jesse in Bethlehem. Samuel, guided by the Lord, went to Jesse's house to fulfill this mission.

When Samuel arrived at Jesse's house, he asked to see Jesse's sons, as one of them was to be anointed as the future king. Jesse presented his seven eldest sons to Samuel, starting with the oldest, but God chose none of them.

Samuel then inquired if Jesse had any more sons, and Jesse mentioned that the youngest, David, was out tending to the sheep. Samuel insisted on seeing David; when David arrived, he was a young and ruddy shepherd. As soon as Samuel saw him, the Lord said to Samuel, "Rise and anoint him, this is the one."

TESTIMONIAL

Samuel anointed David with oil, signifying that God chose him to be the future king of Israel. From that moment on, the Spirit of the Lord came upon David in power. He was not an immediate king, but this anointing marked the beginning of his journey toward fulfilling his destiny as a significant figure in the history of Israel.

David's gift, in this case, was his leadership and kingly potential, which was revealed through Samuel's anointing. Throughout his life, David developed his gifts, such as his musical talent, his expertise as a warrior, and his deep relationship with God, and he eventually became the renowned King David, known for his wisdom, Psalms, and leadership in Israel.

This story serves as an example of someone discovering their God-given gift and embracing their divine calling.

PRAYER GUIDANCE

PRAYER FOR YOUR GIFT

Heavenly Father, I thank You for the unique gifts You have blessed me with. Help me to identify and understand my talents and show me how to use them to serve others and bring glory to Your Name. Lord, I know these gifts are not meant for me alone, but to be shared with the world. Give me the strength and confidence to embrace them fully and the humility to use them for the greater good. Guide me on the path of healing and purpose as I seek to fulfill Your plan for my life through the gifts You have given me, in Jesus' name, I pray.

Amen

In the space provided, offer a prayer to God, seeking His guidance in understanding and using your gifts for His glory:

May this Day 23 entry help you recognize and embrace the gifts God has bestowed upon you and inspire you to use them for His glory and the healing of your heart.

DAY 24

TITLE: <u>Forgiveness</u>   **DATES:** _____

SCRIPTURE REFERENCE

Matthew 6:14-15 (NIV)

"For if you forgive other people when they sin against you, your heavenly Father will also forgive you. But if you do not forgive others their sins, your Father will not forgive your sins."

SPIRITUAL THOUGHT

Think back over the years and your past about who wronged you, hurt you, or broke your heart, etc. Pull from within yourself to forgive them because forgiveness is a decision, and a decision is what you deliberately do. You can find comfort in forgiving others because forgiveness sets you free, and it's for you, not the other person. Always remember that forgiveness is based on a decision. It's not a feeling, it's intentional.

SCRIPTURES OF THE DAY

Draw wisdom, hope, and reassurance from these verses:

"Bear with each other and forgive one another if any of you has a grievance against someone. Forgive as the Lord forgave you."
Colossians 3:13 (NIV)

GUIDED SELF-REFLECTION

Today, let us focus on the theme of forgiveness in our lives. Take a moment to reflect on these questions:

1. Is there someone you need to forgive, either yourself or another person?

----

2. What emotions are associated with this need for forgiveness?

----

3. How has holding onto unforgiveness affected your healing journey so far?

TESTIMONIAL

In Genesis 37-50, you will find the story of Joseph. Joseph, the favorite son of Jacob, is sold into slavery by his jealous brothers because he revealed to them that he had dreams of them bowing down to him. He ends up in Egypt, where he serves as a slave in Potiphar's house, and later is falsely accused of a rape crime by Potiphar's wife and imprisoned for years. Joseph's ability to interpret dreams leads to his release from prison after he interprets Pharoah's dream, resulting in him being appointed as a high-ranking official in Egypt, second only to Pharaoh. He is tasked with preparing Egypt for a severe famine that lasted for seven years.

The famine drives Joseph's brothers to Egypt in search of food. They do not recognize Joseph, as they were standing before him, but he recognized them. Joseph tests his brothers by keeping Simeon in Egypt and demanding they return with their youngest brother, Benjamin. In Genesis 45, Joseph reveals his true identity to his brothers, and they are filled with remorse and fear. Instead of seeking revenge, Joseph forgives them, recognizing God's plan for their actions. He invites his family to come to Egypt for safety and provisions during the famine.

Shortly afterward, Joseph's family settles in Egypt, and there is a reunion with his Father, Jacob; he continues to provide for them during the famine. When Jacob dies, Joseph's brothers worry that he might seek revenge, but Joseph reassures them, saying that what they meant for evil, God meant for good (Genesis 50:20).

TESTIMONIAL

Joseph's journey is a powerful example of forgiveness and the transformative power of God's plan. Despite the betrayal and hardship, he endured, he chose to forgive his brothers, leading to reconciliation and the preservation of his family during a difficult time.

This story illustrates the importance of forgiveness and demonstrates how God can use even the most challenging circumstances for good. As you read and reflect on the story of Joseph and the forgiveness he displayed, remember that you are not alone on this journey, and there is hope in God's healing power for you.

PRAYER GUIDANCE

PRAYER FOR FORGIVENESS

Father, in Jesus' name, let this reflection soften the heart of the one who's seeking forgiveness. Father, I send forth Your Word to bring healing and reconciliation. May the truth and depth of Your love be known and felt. Grant us the grace to forgive as You have forgiven us. Help us release the burdens of resentment and anger and replace them with freedom and peace by extending Your mercy.

In this moment, we place our trust in Your divine plan, believing that through forgiveness, hearts can be mended, and relationships can be restored. May the light of Jesus shine through us as instruments of Your grace. I pray for the strength to let go of past hurts and the courage to embrace the future with love, forgiveness, and understanding. We ask for Your guidance and your unwavering love.

When you choose to forgive, say, "God, I release the person (or people) to you in Jesus' name. I have written about how it made me feel (violated, hurt, angry, etc.). Father, You are the Forgiver of sins, and I lift them up to You. As You forgive me, I aggressively forgive them. God, I release all hurt and brokenness from my heart, humiliation, guilt, and shame. I come out of agreement with these things, and I declare myself free in Jesus' name.

Amen

Put your prayer next and put yourself in a place where you're writing to one person. Title it: "Prayer for Forgiveness."

May this Day 24 entry on forgiveness be a significant step toward mending your heart and embarking on a transformative healing journey. Lean on your faith, self-reflection, and prayerful guidance as you walk along the path to forgiveness and healing.

DAY 25

TITLE: <u>The Power of Prayer</u>   **DATES:** _____

SCRIPTURE REFERENCE

1 Thessalonians 5:17 (ESV)

"Pray without ceasing."

SPIRITUAL THOUGHT

Today, we dive into the profound practice of prayer and its transformative power.

SCRIPTURES OF THE DAY

Draw wisdom and hope from these verses:

"And this is the confidence that we have toward him, that if we ask anything according to his will, he hears us."
1 John 5:14 (ESV)

"The Lord is near to all who call on him, to all who call on him in truth."
Psalm 145:18 (ESV)

GUIDED SELF-REFLECTION

Engage in self-reflection regarding your prayer life:

1. **Your Prayer Journey:** Reflect on your personal journey of prayer. Have you found comfort, strength, or guidance through prayer during your healing journey? Write down your experiences.

----

2. **Challenges in Prayer:** Consider any challenges or doubts you've faced in your prayer life. Have there been moments when you questioned whether God hears your prayers or when you struggled to pray? Reflect on how you navigated those challenges.

----

3. **Growing in Prayer:** What steps can you take to deepen your prayer life and make it an integral part of your healing journey? How can you nurture your connection with God through prayer?

TESTIMONIAL

One of the prominent biblical stories that revolve around prayer is the story of Daniel and the lion's den. This story can be found in Daniel Chapter 6.

During this time, Daniel was a high-ranking official in the kingdom of Babylon under the rule of King Darius. His position and integrity had made him well-known among the people. However, out of jealousy and spite, some of the other officials conspired against him. They knew Daniel was a devout man who faithfully prayed to his God three times a day.

These officials devised a plan to trap Daniel by convincing King Darius to issue a decree that forbade anyone from making petitions to any god or man for thirty days except to the king himself. Unaware of their ulterior motives, the king agreed to the decree and signed it into law.

Despite the king's decree, Daniel continued to pray to his God as before. When his enemies discovered Daniel praying, they reported it to King Darius, who was greatly distressed because he valued Daniel and did not want to see him punished. However, because the king had signed the decree, he was bound by his own law and had to order that Daniel be cast into a den of lions.

TESTIMONIAL

Before Daniel was thrown into the lion's den, King Darius expressed his hope that Daniel's God would deliver him. After a night of fasting and distress, the king returned to the den the next morning and found Daniel alive and unharmed.

Daniel explained that God had sent an angel to shut the mouths of the lions, sparing his life.

This story emphasizes the power of prayer and faith in the face of adversity. Daniel's unwavering commitment to his daily prayers demonstrated his trust in God despite the threat to his life. His faith led to a miraculous intervention where God's protection was clearly evident.

The story of Daniel and the lion's den illustrates the importance of prayer as a means of seeking guidance, strength, and deliverance in challenging situations, and it also highlights the theme of divine protection for the faithful.

PRAYER GUIDANCE

PRAYER FOR THE POWER OF PRAYER

Lord, I come before You today with a heart full of gratitude for the gift of prayer. You've been my refuge, my Source of strength, and my Guide on this healing journey. I acknowledge the challenges I've faced in my prayer life and ask for Your guidance and grace to overcome them. Help me to deepen my connection with You through consistent and heartfelt prayer. May my prayers be a source of healing, understanding, and comfort as I continue on this journey of restoration. I place my faith in the power of prayer in Jesus' name.

Amen

In the space provided, offer a prayer to God, expressing your thoughts and feelings about prayer and seeking His guidance:

May this Day 25 entry deepen your appreciation for the power of prayer and encourage you to make it a central part of your healing journey.

DAY 26

TITLE: <u>The Gift of Praise</u>　　　　　　**DATES:** _____

SCRIPTURE REFERENCE

Hebrews 13:15 (KJV)

"Pray without ceasing."

SPIRITUAL THOUGHT

Today, we focus on the power of praise and how it can uplift our
spirits.

SCRIPTURES OF THE DAY

Draw inspiration from these verses:

"The Lord is my strength and my shield; in him my heart trusts,
and I am helped; my heart exults, and with my song, I give thanks
to him."
Psalm 28:7 (ESV)

"Let everything that has breath praise the Lord! Praise the Lord!"
Psalm 150:6 (ESV)

GUIDED SELF-REFLECTION

Reflect on the role of praise in your life:

1. **The Joy of Praise:** Have there been moments in your life when you've experienced the joy and comfort that comes from praising God? Write about those moments.

----

2. **Challenges in Praising:** Consider any challenges you've faced in offering praise, especially during difficult times. How have you navigated those challenges?

----

3. **Making Praise a Habit:** What steps can you take to make praise a consistent practice in your life? How can praise become a source of strength and healing on your journey?

TESTIMONIAL

 A story that revolves around praise is the story of Paul and Silas in the Philippian jail, which can be found in Acts 16:16-40.

In this story, Paul and Silas, two early Christian missionaries, were in the city of Philippi. They were spreading the message of Christianity when they encountered a slave girl who was possessed by a spirit of divination. This girl had been making money for her owners by fortune-telling. She began to follow Paul and Silas, shouting that they were servants of the Most High God who proclaimed the way of salvation.

Although what the girl said was true, and because she did this for days, Paul was greatly annoyed by her constant shouting, so, in the Name of Jesus, he cast the spirit out of her. This action resulted in her owners losing their source of income, leading to their anger and frustration.

The owners seized Paul and Silas and brought them before the local authorities, accusing them of causing trouble in the city. The crowd joined in the accusations. The magistrates stripped Paul and Silas and ordered that they be beaten and thrown into prison. The jailer was instructed to guard them securely.

TESTIMONIAL

Despite the harsh conditions in the inner prison and their physical suffering, Paul and Silas responded with praise and prayer. Acts 16:25-26 describes the scene:

"But about midnight, Paul and Silas were praying and singing hymns to God, and the prisoners were listening to them, and suddenly there was a great earthquake so that the foundations of the prison were shaken. And immediately, all the doors were opened, and everyone's bonds were unfastened."

The earthquake miraculously set the prisoners free, but Paul and Silas chose to stay and prevent the jailer from taking his own life, as he thought all the prisoners had escaped. The jailer was deeply moved by their actions and asked how he could be saved. In response, Paul and Silas shared the message of Jesus with him, and the jailer and his household accepted the Christian faith.

This story illustrates how, even in the midst of adversity and imprisonment, Paul and Silas chose to praise and pray to God. Their faith and worship in difficult circumstances led to miraculous events and the conversion of the jailer, highlighting the power of praise.

PRAYER GUIDANCE

PRAYER FOR THE GIFT OF PRAISE

Dear Heavenly Father, I lift my voice in praise and gratitude today. You are the Source of my strength and my healing. I've witnessed the transformation that comes from offering praise, even in challenging times. I acknowledge the moments when praise has lifted my spirit and brought me closer to You. Yet, I've also faced moments when praise seemed difficult. Grant me the grace to make praise a consistent practice, a wellspring of strength and healing. May my praises be a sweet offering to You and a source of peace on this healing journey. I embrace the gift of praise in Jesus' name.

Amen

In the space provided, offer a prayer to God, expressing your thoughts and feelings about praise and seeking His guidance:

May this Day 26 entry remind you of the gift of praise and inspire you to continue practicing on your healing journey.

DAY 27
TITLE: <u>The Power of Worship</u>   **DATES:** _____

SCRIPTURE REFERENCE

John 4:24 (KJV)

"God is a Spirit: and they that worship him must worship him in spirit and in truth."

SPIRITUAL THOUGHT

Today, we explore the healing power of worship and its ability to mend our hearts.

SCRIPTURES OF THE DAY

Direct your reflection on these verses:

"O come, let us worship and bow down: let us kneel before the Lord our maker."
Psalm 95:6 (KJV)

"Ascribe to the Lord the glory due his name; worship the Lord in the splendor of his holiness."
Psalm 29:2 (NIV)

GUIDED SELF-REFLECTION

Reflect on your relationship with worship:

1. **Defining Worship:** What does worship mean to you? How do you engage in worship in your daily life, both individually and collectively?

----

2. **Moments of Connection:** Recall times when worship has brought you a sense of connection, comfort, or healing. Write about these moments.

----

3. **Making Worship a Habit:** What steps can you take to make worship a regular part of your life and your healing journey?

TESTIMONIAL

A biblical story that deals with worship is the account of the Wise Men, who came to worship the infant Jesus. This story is found in the Gospel of Matthew 2:1-12. The story of the Wise Men begins with their journey from the East to Jerusalem, having observed a star that signified the birth of a significant king. They arrived in Jerusalem and inquired about the location of the child who had been born "King of the Jews." Their question troubled King Herod and all of Jerusalem.

Herod summoned the chief priests and scribes to inquire about the birthplace of the Messiah, and they pointed to Bethlehem as the prophesied location. Herod then secretly met with the Wise Men, asking them to find the child and report back to him so that he, too, could go and worship him.

The Wise Men continued their journey to Bethlehem, and the star they had been following led them to the house where Jesus and his family were. Upon seeing the child, they were filled with joy and fell down to worship him. They presented gifts of gold, frankincense, and myrrh to the baby Jesus as tokens of their adoration.

TESTIMONIAL

In this story, the Wise Men's journey to find and worship the newborn Jesus symbolizes the act of seeking and acknowledging His divine presence. Their worship reflects the recognition of Jesus as a significant figure and the fulfillment of Messianic prophecies.

The presentation of gifts was a form of worship and tribute, as gold symbolized Jesus' royalty, frankincense represented his divinity, and myrrh was used for anointing, foreshadowing his sacrificial death.

The story of the Wise Men's worship of Jesus is significant, emphasizing the idea that Jesus is worthy of worship and adoration, not only by those who knew him at the time, but also by all who come to recognize Him as the Savior and the King. It serves as a reminder of the importance of worship and the acknowledgment of Jesus as the central figure of faith.

PRAYER GUIDANCE

PRAYER FOR WORSHIP

Father, as I reflect on the power of worship, I am reminded of the deep connection it brings, the comfort it provides, and the healing it offers. I find strength in knowing that worship allows me to draw near to You. Help me define worship in my own life and cultivate it as a healing practice. May it be a source of comfort and a reminder of Your presence. I open my heart to the amazing power of worship, in Jesus' name.

Amen

In the space provided, offer a prayer to God, expressing your thoughts and feelings about worship and seeking His guidance:

May this Day 27 entry encourage you to embrace the power of worship and make it an integral part of your healing journey.

DAY 28
TITLE: <u>Celebrating Breakthrough</u>   DATES:_____

SCRIPTURE REFERENCE

Isaiah 43:19 (KJV)

"Behold, I will do a new thing; now it shall spring forth; shall ye not know it? I will even make a way in the wilderness, and rivers in the desert."

SPIRITUAL THOUGHT

Today, let us focus on celebrating the breakthrough moments in our healing journey.

SCRIPTURES OF THE DAY

Find inspiration and strength in these verses:

"Behold, I am doing a new thing; now it springs forth, do you not perceive it? I will make a way in the wilderness and rivers in the desert."
Isaiah 43:19 (ESV)

"And we know that in all things God works for the good of those who love him, who have been called according to his purpose."
Romans 8:28 (NIV)

GUIDED SELF-REFLECTION

Reflect on the concept of breakthrough:

1. **Your Breakthroughs:** Take a moment to recall and celebrate the breakthroughs you've experienced on your healing journey. These could be moments of clarity, strength, or emotional release. Write about what these breakthroughs mean to you.

----

2. **Obstacles Overcome:** Identify the obstacles or challenges you've overcome on this journey. How have they shaped you and contributed to your growth?

----

3. **Expecting Future Breakthroughs:** What breakthroughs are you hoping for in the future? How do you envision them? Write down your goals.

TESTIMONIAL

In 2 Kings 4:1-7, a widow came to the prophet Elisha for help. Her husband, who was one of the sons of the prophets, had died, leaving her with debts and creditors threatening to take her two sons as slaves to settle the debts. The widow was in a terrible situation and had nothing except a jar of oil.

Elisha asked her what she had in her house, and she mentioned the jar of oil. Elisha then instructed her to go and borrow as many empty vessels as she could from her neighbors. Once she had gathered the empty vessels, she was told to pour the small amount of oil she had into these vessels.

As the widow followed Elisha's instructions, and began to pour the oil, a miraculous breakthrough occurred. The small jar of oil kept pouring and filling the borrowed vessels until all of them were full. Elisha then instructed her to sell the oil, pay off her debts, and use the remaining funds to provide for herself and her sons.

This story of the widow and the miracle of the oil demonstrates how God can provide a breakthrough in times of desperation. The widow's obedience to the prophet's instructions and her faith led to the multiplication of her oil, which enabled her to overcome her financial crisis and secure a future for her family. This serves as a powerful illustration of God's ability to bring about breakthroughs and deliverance, even in seemingly hopeless situations.

PRAYER GUIDANCE

PRAYER FOR CELEBRATING BREAKTHROUGH

Father, I thank You for the breakthroughs on my healing journey. They are reminders of Your power and your faithfulness. I celebrate the obstacles I've overcome, knowing they have contributed to my growth. As I look to the future, I seek Your guidance and strength for future breakthroughs. May Your presence be a constant source of hope and renewal. I trust in Your plan for my life in Jesus' name.

Amen

In the space provided, offer a prayer to God, expressing your gratitude for the breakthroughs you've experienced and your future breakthroughs:

May this Day 28 entry be a celebration of the breakthroughs in your life and a reminder that more is on the way as you continue your healing journey.

DAY 29

TITLE: <u>Receiving Healing</u>   **DATES:** _____

SCRIPTURE REFERENCE

Psalm 147:3 (NIV)

"He heals the brokenhearted and binds up their wounds."

SPIRITUAL THOUGHT

Today, let us move into the profound journey of healing and the divine promise of restoration.

SCRIPTURES OF THE DAY

Anchor your healing process in these comforting verses:

"But he was wounded for our transgressions, he was bruised for our iniquities: the chastisement of our peace was upon him; and with his stripes, we are healed."
Isaiah 53:5 (KJV)

"The Lord is close to the brokenhearted and saves those who are crushed in spirit."
Psalm 34:18 (NIV)

GUIDED SELF-REFLECTION

Reflect on your Healing Journey:

1 **Recognizing Healing:** Take a moment to acknowledge the areas in your life where you've experienced healing. What have you already healed from? Write down the emotions and experiences tied to these healing moments.

----

2. **Divine Healing:** Consider the role of your faith in the healing process. How has your relationship with God and your faith impacted your journey? Write about the comfort and strength you've found in your faith.

----

3. **Embracing Ongoing Healing:** Healing is an ongoing journey. What areas of your life do you feel still need healing? How do you envision your healing journey continuing? Write about your aspirations for continued healing.

TESTIMONIAL

One of the well-known biblical stories that deal with inner healing or healing is the account of Jesus healing the woman with a hemorrhage and raising Jairus's daughter from the dead. This story can be found in the Gospels of Mark (Mark 5:21-43) and Luke (Luke 8:40-56).

In this story, Jairus, a synagogue leader, came to Jesus and begged Him to come to his house because his daughter, who was 12 years old, was gravely ill and near death. Jesus agreed to go with Jairus to heal his daughter.

As they were on their way to Jairus's house, a large crowd pressed around Jesus. In the midst of the crowd was a woman who had been suffering with an issue of blood for twelve years. She had spent all her money on doctors but had not found relief from her condition. In her desperation, she believed that if she could just touch the hem of Jesus' garment, she would be healed.

As the woman reached out and touched the fringe of Jesus' robe, she was instantly healed. Jesus felt power go out from Him and asked who had touched Him. The woman, trembling with fear and awe, came forward to explain what had happened. Jesus responded with compassion and told her that her faith had made her well.

TESTIMONIAL

While this encounter was taking place, messengers arrived and informed Jairus that his daughter had died. However, Jesus encouraged Jairus to have faith and continued to his house. When they arrived, Jesus entered the room where the girl laid and took her by the hand. He spoke to her, saying, "Talitha cumi," which means, "Little girl, I say to you, arise!" The girl immediately came back to life.

This story illustrates the healing power of Jesus and the importance of faith. The woman with the issue of blood found inner healing from her suffering through her faith in Jesus. At the same time, Jairus and his family experienced the profound healing of their daughter's physical and spiritual well-being. It emphasizes that through faith, and trust in Jesus, even the most desperate situations can be healed and transformed.

PRAYER GUIDANCE

PRAYER FOR RECEIVING HEALING

Heavenly Father, I come before You with a heart filled with gratitude for the healing I've experienced on this journey. Your promise to heal the brokenhearted is a source of comfort and strength. As I continue on this path, I seek Your guidance and your healing touch in the areas of my life that still need restoration. I trust in Your divine plan for my healing. I pray for ongoing healing and restoration in Jesus' name.

Amen

In the space provided, offer a prayer to God, expressing your gratitude for the healing you've experienced and seeking His guidance and continued healing:

May this Day 29 entry remind you of the healing you've experienced and inspire you to embrace the ongoing journey toward wholeness with faith and courage.

DAY 30
TITLE: <u>Embracing Restoration</u>   DATES:_____

SCRIPTURE REFERENCE

Joel 2:25 (ESV)

"I will restore to you the years that the swarming locust has eaten, the hopper, the destroyer, and the cutter, my great army, which I sent among you."

SPIRITUAL THOUGHT

As we conclude this journey, let us focus on the promise of restoration and God's ability to mend what was broken.

SCRIPTURES OF THE DAY

Anchor your restoration journey in these comforting verses:

"He restores my soul. He leads me on the path of righteousness for his name's sake"
Psalm 23:3 (ESV)

"For I know the plans I have for you, declares the Lord, plans for welfare and not for evil, to give you a future and a hope."
Jeremiah 29:11 (ESV)

GUIDED SELF-REFLECTION

Reflect on your journey towards restoration

1. **Acknowledging Restoration:** Take time to recognize the areas of your life where you've already experienced restoration. What have you reclaimed? Write down the emotions and experiences related to these restorative moments.

----

2. **God's Role in Restoration:** Consider the role of God in the restoration process. How has your faith and your relationship with God contributed to your restoration? Write about the grace and mercy you've found in your faith.

----

3. **Continued Restoration:** Restoration is a continuous journey. What areas of your life still await restoration? How do you envision God's restoration continuing in your life? Write about your hopes for ongoing restoration.

TESTIMONIAL

The story of Job is an insightful narrative that ultimately deals with restoration, but it also involves a significant journey of suffering and faith before reaching that point.

Job was a man known for his faithfulness, righteousness, and wealth. He was described as "blameless" and "upright" before God. However, satan challenged Job's faith, arguing that he was righteous only because he had been blessed with good wealth. In a test allowed by God, satan brought immense suffering upon Job, taking away his wealth, health, and even the lives of his children.

Job's suffering was intense, and he wrestled with deep questions and doubts about God's justice and wisdom. He had friends who attempted to provide explanations for his suffering, but their advice was often simplistic and unhelpful. Despite his severe struggles, Job maintained his integrity and did not curse God.

The story of Job then deals with a period of serious dialogue between Job and his friends and God Himself. Job questioned the nature of suffering and God's reasons for allowing it. His friends offered numerous explanations but could not satisfy Job's deep need for understanding.

TESTIMONIAL

Finally, in Job chapters 38-42, God responded directly to Job, addressing his questions and concerns. God's response emphasized His infinite wisdom, creative power, and sovereignty over all creation. Job was humbled by God's presence and inability to fully comprehend the great purposes.

As for the theme of restoration, the story of Job ends with God's restoration of Job's fortunes. In Job 42:10-17, we read that after Job had endured his trials and humbled himself before God, the Lord restored his prosperity and blessed him with even greater wealth and a new family. Job's story emphasizes God's ultimate sovereignty and the importance of persevering through suffering and maintaining faith, even when we don't fully understand the reasons behind our trials.

Job's story is a powerful illustration of God's ability to restore and bless those who endure suffering and maintain their faith, even in the face of profound challenges and questions about the nature of suffering and God's justice. It reminds us of the importance of trusting in God's wisdom and sovereignty, even when we cannot fathom the reasons for our trials.

PRAYER GUIDANCE

PRAYER FOR EMBRACING RESTORATION

Father, I stand before You with a heart full of gratitude for the restoration I've experienced on this journey. Your promise to restore what was lost is a source of hope and joy. As I move forward, I seek Your help and continued restoration in the areas of my life that still need it. I trust in Your plan for my restoration. I pray for ongoing restoration and fulfilling Your plans for my future in Jesus' name.

Amen

In the space provided, offer a prayer to God, expressing your gratitude for the restoration you've experienced and seeking His continued help and restoration:

May this Day 30 entry serve as a reminder of the restoration you've witnessed and inspire you to embrace the ongoing journey toward a future filled with hope and God's restoration.

DAY 31

TITLE: <u>Rejoicing in Victory</u>   **DATES:_____**

SCRIPTURE REFERENCE

1 Corinthians 15:57 (ESV)

"But thanks be to God, who gives us the victory through our Lord
Jesus Christ."

SPIRITUAL THOUGHT

As we close this chapter of your healing journey, let us reflect on
the victory that faith brings.

SCRIPTURES OF THE DAY

Anchor your thoughts in these reassuring verses:

"For the LORD your God is the one who goes with you to fight for
you against your enemies to give you victory."
Deuteronomy 20:4 (NIV)

"I can do all things through him who strengthens me."
Philippians 4:13 (ESV)

GUIDED SELF-REFLECTION

Reflect on the victory you've found in your faith and healing journey:

1. **Recognizing Victories:** Take time to acknowledge the victories you've achieved throughout this journey. What have you overcome? Write about the challenges you've conquered and the emotional growth you've experienced.

----

2. **Faith's Role in Victory:** Consider how your faith has played a crucial role in your victories. How has your relationship with God empowered you to triumph over adversity? Write about the strength and courage you've found through your faith.

----

3. **Continued Victories:** Victory is an ongoing process. Reflect on areas of your life where you still aspire to achieve victory. How do you envision your faith leading you to further triumph? Write about your hopes and aspirations for continued victories.

TESTIMONIAL

One of the stories that deals with victory is the story of David and Goliath, found in 1 Samuel 17.

The story of David and Goliath takes place during the time when the Israelites were facing the Philistines in a fierce battle. The Philistines had a giant warrior named Goliath who challenged the Israelites to send out a champion to engage in single combat. Goliath's size, strength, and intimidating presence struck fear into the hearts of the Israelite soldiers, and they were reluctant to accept his challenge.

David, a young shepherd who was not yet a soldier, came to the Israelite camp to visit his brothers and bring them food. When he heard Goliath's taunts and saw the fear in the faces of the Israelite soldiers, he offered to face Goliath. King Saul, impressed by David's confidence, allowed him to do so.

David refused to wear traditional armor and instead took only a sling and five smooth stones from the brook. With great faith in God, David faced Goliath. He placed a stone in his sling and struck Goliath in the forehead, causing the giant to fall to the ground. David then took Goliath's own sword and beheaded him, securing victory for the Israelites.

TESTIMONIAL

The victory of David over Goliath is often seen as a symbol of triumph against apparent overwhelming odds through faith and trust in God. It highlights the importance of courage, faith, and reliance on God's strength in the face of adversity. David's victory exemplifies how even the weakest can overcome the strongest when they have faith in the Lord and His power. This story has become a source of inspiration for those facing intimidating challenges and serves as a reminder that victory is possible with God on our side.

PRAYER GUIDANCE

PRAYER FOR REJOICING IN VICTORY

Father, I come before You with a heart filled with gratitude for the victories, I've achieved on this healing journey. Your grace has been my source of strength. As I move forward, I seek Your help and inspiration to continue achieving victories in all areas of my life. I trust in Your plans and Your strength. I pray for the courage to face new challenges with unwavering faith and achieve victory in Jesus' name.

Amen

In the space provided, offer a prayer to God, expressing gratitude for the victories you've achieved and seeking His continued direction and encouragement for the future:

May this Day 31 entry serve as a reminder of the victories you've attained and inspire you to embrace the future with faith, courage, and confidence in God's plans for you.

CONCLUSION

In closing, this journal has been a blessed and transforming 31-day journey, inviting you to explore the depths of your emotional cup and guiding you to fill it with the profound blessings of faith, love, and healing.

You have discovered the power of surrender, renewal, and connection with the Father through faith-based reflections, guided self-reflection, scriptures, personal testimonials, and prayerful guidance.

As you move forward from these pages, may your heart be mended, your spirit renewed, and your faith deepened. With the grace of God, your journey continues, and the path of healing and hope remains before you.

JOURNAL NOTES

JOURNAL NOTES

JOURNAL NOTES

JOURNAL NOTES

ABOUT THE AUTHOR

LaShana Lloyd is a Christian author, writer, blogger, speaker, and life coach for women. She serves women who have gone through painful, traumatic experiences by using inner healing techniques to help them regain their wholeness. Her mission is to prepare women worldwide by inspiring and encouraging them to walk purposely in their calling for God. She is the founder and owner of Faith Led Life, LLC, where she teaches women how to uncover hidden challenges that may be sabotaging their purpose so that they can live the life God intended them to live.

LaShana was featured in the bestselling book anthology titled "You Have No Idea the Hell I've Been Through: 22 Women Who Pushed from Pain to Purpose," She also released "What's Blocking Your Confidence? Effective Ways to Conquer Your Fears (Second Edition) in 2022."

LaShana is originally from Clio, South Carolina, but currently resides in Tampa Bay, Florida.

Learn more about LaShana at www.faithledlife.com

CONNECT WITH ME

To contact the author for book speaking engagements, bulk purchases, or comments, please reach out to:

Website: www.faithledlife.com

Email: info@faithledlife.com

Social Media

Facebook @ faithledlifeofficial

LinkedIn @ faithledlife

Pinterest @ faithledlife

Twitter @ FaithLedLife

X @ faithledlifeofficial

Clubhouse @ faithledlife

www.ingramcontent.com/pod-product-compliance
Lightning Source LLC
Chambersburg PA
CBHW051157120626
46547CB00012B/1098